ARTS AND ACADEMIA

Great Debates in Higher Education is a series of short, accessible books addressing key challenges to and issues in Higher Education, on a national and international level. These books are research informed but debate driven. They are intended to be relevant to a broad spectrum of researchers, students and administrators in higher education, and are designed to help us unpick and assess the state of higher education systems, policies, and social and economic impacts.

Higher Education at the Crossroads of Disruption: The University
of the 21st Century
Andreas Kaplan

Combatting Marginalisation by Co-Creating Education: Methods,
Theories and Practices From the Perspectives of Young People
*Edited by David Thore Gravesen, Kaz Stuart, Mette Bunting, Sidse
Hølvig Mikkelsen and Peter Hornbæk Frostholm*

Challenging the Teaching Excellence Framework: Diversity Deficits
in Higher Education Evaluations
Amanda French and Kate Carruthers Thomas

Leadership of Historically Black Colleges and Universities: A What
Not to Do Guide for HBCU Leaders
Johnny D. Jones

The Fully Functioning University
Tom Bourner, Asher Rospigliosi and Linda Heath

A Brief History of Credit in UK Higher Education: Laying Siege to
the Ivory Tower
Wayne Turnbull

Degendering Leadership in Higher Education
Barret Katuna

Cultural Journeys in Higher Education: Student Voices and
Narratives
Jan Bamford and Lucy Pollard

Perspectives on Access to Higher Education
Sam Broadhead, Rosemarie Davis and Anthony Hudson

Radicalisation and Counter-Radicalisation in Higher Education
Catherine McGlynn and Shaun McDaid

Refugees in Higher Education: Debate, Discourse and Practice
Jacqueline Stevenson and Sally Baker

The Marketisation of English Higher Education: A Policy Analysis of a Risk-Based System
Colin McCaig

Access to Success and Social Mobility Through Higher Education: A Curate's Egg?
Edited by Stuart Billingham

Evaluating Scholarship and Research Impact: History, Practices, and Policy Development
Jeffrey W. Alstete, Nicholas J. Beutell and John P. Meyer

Sexual Violence on Campus: Power-Conscious Approaches to Awareness, Prevention, and Response
Chris Linder

Higher Education, Access and Funding: The UK in International Perspective
Edited by Sheila Riddell, Sarah Minty, Elisabet Weedon and Susan Whittaker

British Universities in the Brexit Moment: Political, Economic and Cultural Implications
Mike Finn

Teaching Excellence in Higher Education: Challenges, Changes and the Teaching Excellence Framework
Amanda French and Matt O'Leary

ARTS AND ACADEMIA

The Role of the Arts in Civic Universities

BY

CAROLA BOEHM
Staffordshire University, UK

United Kingdom – North America – Japan
India – Malaysia – China

Emerald Publishing Limited
Howard House, Wagon Lane, Bingley BD16 1WA, UK

First edition 2022

British Library Cataloguing in Publication Data
A catalogue record for this book is available from the British Library

ISBN: 978-1-83867-730-5 (Print)
ISBN: 978-1-83867-727-5 (Online)
ISBN: 978-1-83867-729-9 (Epub)

ISOQAR certified
Management System,
awarded to Emerald
for adherence to
Environmental
standard
ISO 14001:2004.

ISOQAR
REGISTERED
Certificate Number 1985
ISO 14001

INVESTOR IN PEOPLE

I dedicate this book to all creatives and academics passionate about the role of arts and culture in our society.

TABLE OF CONTENTS

LIST OF FIGURES, TABLES AND TABLEAUS

LIST OF ABBREVIATIONS

ACE   Arts Council England
CMA   Competition and Markets Authority
CPE   Cultural Political Economy
DCMS   Department of Digital, Culture, Media and Sports
EDI   Equality, Diversity and Inclusion
GVA   Gross Value Added
HE   Higher Education
HEI   Higher Education Institution
HESA   Higher Education Statistics Agency
KEF   Knowledge Excellence Framework
OfS   Office for Students
PaR   Practice-as-Research
PLC   Public Liability Company
PPL   Phonographic Performance Limited
PRS   Performing Right Society and Mechanical-Copyright Protection Society
QAA   Quality Assurance Agency
R&D   Research and Development
RAE   Research Assessment Exercise
RDI   Research, Development and Innovation
REF   Research Excellence Framework
TEF   Teaching Excellence Framework
UE15   The 15 member states of the European Union before enlargement in 2004

FOREWORD

This book is about the delightful nooks and crannies of where art finds itself in academia, exploring questions of where art lives in the university sector and how it interacts with the outside, how it reaches beyond its boundaries.

And as I am writing these passages, or rather adding to the book's content which had been relatively stable until 2019 when the pandemic appeared on all of our horizons, I find myself going through the entire content and adapting it to a post-pandemic view of the world. And whilst I am changing all verbs from present tense or simple past to past perfect, amending policy references to denote the political and social rupture, with various flingings onto the pile of policies made irrelevant by the pandemic, adding sections to make sense of the truth in a completely new crises moment in modern history, I realise how the matter of this book has become even more important.

This book was largely conceptualised pre-COVID, at a time when the belief in the power of rationality seemed under constant threat – and with it, our universities' core knowledge-related activities in understanding what it means to be human. And my personal belief was that when rationality seemed to stop working, art can reach on an emotional level, important to ensure our messages have reach and impact, and thus arts in Higher Education became increasingly important as it contributed so heavily to the essence of what it meant to be human.

But this pandemic horrifically gave us back an urgent sense of the need for rationality, experiencing on a daily basis how various nations relied heavily on their scientists to steer us through this calamitous moment. Facts and scientific statistics, presented regularly in governmental press briefings, provided one of the strongest arguments for us all needing to understand the importance of experts, research and the need to scrutinise, reflect and interrogate the world of facts in order to embed its implications in policies that are geared towards keeping us all safe.

Simultaneously, a locked-down public came together in diverse virtual worlds to keep sane through creative engagements, artistic tasks and active cultural participation online. The number of audiences reaching for smartphones, laptops and computers to access arts and culture exploded, and creative and cultural professionals stepped up to support access to engaging and transformational arts activities in a multitude of diverse ways.

In my words, governmental pandemic policies might have kept us safe, but arts and culture kept us sane.

However, the long tail-end of the age of post-truth un-rationality, and its potential international impact, kept us up during the 3 November 2021 US presidential elections. It provided a brusque awakening on the day after the end of the Brexit transition period on 31 December 2020 and its related EU-UK Trade and Cooperation Agreements (TCA) and shocked us with the 6 January 2021 US Capitol Riots.

The latter will, in my opinion, end up representing the climax of a moment in time where the post-truth era reared its ugly head and let us know how long-term damage can be wrought when we, in our respective societies, do not attend to nurturing critical reflection in our educational systems, when we ignore to assure our social connectivity mechanisms are fit for purpose and maintain diversity in our public democratic spaces. This rupture of our global community has come at a time where in all its bleakness, it also provided a slimmer of hope that we might utilise to rethink how we might come back stronger, more resilient and more sustainable. What should a green, creative and resilient recovery look like?

We live in this time, a time where we – as the earth's most thinking and creative species – have to overcome our own man-made, most pernicious ecological challenges. This was happening – apparently coincidentally, but we know it to be very much linked – to a time when a substantial part of our society seemed to discount that same rationality and critical thinking which would allow us to solve the growing number of disruptions in the political, economic, societal, as well as ecological sphere.

And from the place where I am writing, in the United Kingdom, during 10 years of Hunger Game austerity and three years of Brexit Blindness, and then more than one year of COVID-19 calamity, the government still seems to be struggling to understand the role and value of universities for our future societies and relying on its chumocracy and a hyper-marketised ideology, failing continually to resolve the most pernicious problems that the natural world is throwing at us currently.

Pre-COVID-19, overarching policy and regulatory frameworks seemed to afford a risk-minimising conformity rather than innovation-resulting experimentation, contrary to various explicitly formulated policy aims, thus simply demonstrating some helpless flailing as part of the adding to the layer cake of various failed policy interventions. During COVID-19, the risks to individual's vulnerabilities and whole sectors became even more substantive. The result of this we will feel in decades to come, both in terms of family members lost to the pandemic and our economic situation in a post-pandemic and post-Brexit and pre-climate catastrophe UK world.

In 2019 I wrote that at the heart of the then Higher Education policy thinking seemed to be the simple and basic question of how we can make our universities more impactful whilst not breaking the bank (Boehm, 2019a). This would be a relatively benign way of representing a political and ministerial mindset in which our universities have increasingly become the scapegoat of choice, as David Sweeney suggested in December 2017 at a SRHE (Society for Research into Higher Education) conference keynote. Over the years, various government officials seemed to have washed their hands of the responsibility for the mess in which our nation finds itself, comprehensively outlined in George Monbiot 2016's journalistic explorations of class, inequality, environment, growth obsessions and financial crises (Monbiot, 2016) or Brown's academic analysis of *The Inequality Crisis* (Brown, 2017). Perhaps exactly because universities are one of the few sufficiently 'public' funded institutions left that cover the whole country, they have increasingly been the focus of ministers, allergic against anything statehood-ly, wanting to turn the last available public levers to make all of our nation's miseries disappear.

And this process of scapegoating continued through the pandemic era, as government ministers were too quick to blame anyone but their leadership in safeguarding their own standing. Focus from universities drifted elsewhere at times, though, as the number of scapegoats increased. From blaming returning students for spreading the virus, blaming schools for not delivering adequate online learning, blaming civil servants in slowing interventions down, to blaming the public for loving their freedom too much.

So as much as I would like to bounce the blame back to the gaggle of fast-changing ministers in Westminster to solve the misery that they have created, I do passionately believe that universities are the key to ensuring that our future societies will cope with the substantial challenges ahead (Boehm, 2019b).

And one of the reasons for my confidence (or possibly desperate hope) lies in the knowledge of universities holding that magic ingredient that allows us to fix various fissures in our broken societies, that potent magic glue found in the power of arts and creativity. We seem to live at the end of the long era of modernity, the long end of the age of enlightenment, a tail-end increasingly tainted by a darkness where we had stopped trusting in the power of rationality. It is a point in our social evolution where we still just remember how we trusted in the power of facts, the power of knowledge, and with it the role that universities as knowledge patrons held. But that trust had fragmented to such an extent that politicians and critics (and even our own academic art philosophers) were even questioning why we needed experts and universities in the first place, and so the education editor of *The Times* reported that

> *Sir Roger Scruton, the philosopher and writer, has said that getting rid of universities would be a way of ending the discrimination faced by conservatives on many campuses. He said that universities were state-sponsored institutions and that the hostility faced by conservatives indicated that "we have completely lost control".*
>
> *(Bennett, 2019)*

With this distrust came the forces that we in Higher Education all experienced, pushing universities into the form of workforce production industries, all geared towards – what I would suggest – becoming neoliberal fantasies of globally sovereign markets to the detriment of the health and well-being of our societies all around us.

However, this pandemic gave us a halting point in this neo-liberal, unhinged trajectory built upon decades of high individualism without sufficient balancing with a critical mass of collectivism. Pre-COVID, discussions increasingly centred on the reasons for the demise of our democratic institutions in the era of Trump and Brexit, and whether we were experiencing the end of the age of reason. This pre-COVID era included how our current realities were shocked and shaken by the likes of Brexit and Trump, including the existence of inhumane detention centres, the ad hoc-ness of the Windrush Scandal and constant failings to adhere to basic human rights, all providing an environment where science and facts seemed to not be sufficient anymore to turn minds and hearts of our democratically elected representative towards leading us (ideally with integrity) towards a more sustainable common shared wealth and well-being.

We lived in a time where rationality, science and evidence seemed not enough.

But the pandemic, through its deep disruption, has also brought new ways of thinking to the fore, struggling with the old ideologies. From reconsidering what the future world of work needs to look like, from understanding the effective impacts of nationally different socially oriented approaches to the pandemic, from reconsidering our basic fabric of society, our buildings and what we use these for, and what a sustainable and environmentally recovered society could look like.

But these debates struggle with the political reality of the governments of the day, formed from a pre-pandemic age, still immersed in climate catastrophe denial, British superiority and class inequality and with all that still situated in a politically deeply divided society with regressive electoral tendencies pushing us down various existential dead ends.

We still live in an era where the partisanship of political life has become so divided that it made way for, as an example, the political expediency of a Mitch McConnell (US) (McConnell, 2016), legis-latively enabling the corporate influence into electoral systems in order to retain political power above all else, or the disdainful pragmatism of a Dominic Cummings (UK) (Wikipedia Contribu-tors, 2019) allowing voter manipulation within a referendum as an acceptable means to achieve an end. This is also mirrored by an electorate who have – to a scarily large proportion – encultured and normalised the attitudes of politicians wanting to be on the winning side, no matter the cost, 'do or die' (Boris Johnson on TalkRadio, 2019), taking the right to be right by brute force rather than being right, as the Capitol Riots in January 2021 have shown.

When starting this book, in my introductory paragraph, I expressed my hope that by the time this book was published, some of the chaos and uncertainty and distrust for our political systems would have dissipated. My assumptions were simultaneously right and wrong; right that we were seeing sudden shifts in debates – completely new alternative futures that before had been considered unrealistic and delusional. But wrong that we had reached the pinnacle of chaos, and I had come to accept that this would be a long, painful slog for humanity to work itself back from the brink of catastrophe.

And this struggle between the forces that see only short-term gain, such as acceptance of climate apartheid or vaccine nationalism or a failed economic system, I believe will keep us busy for the rest of the century. And as the world continues to burn and shudder, and the political discourses, at least in this country, kept themselves busy with discourses around economic superiority and sovereignty (and this word has a complex underbelly), I have continually found myself asking what cuts through the fog (see also Boehm, 2019b).

I always thought that this is where the power of the creative arts comes in. When rationality has stopped working, art can reach on an emotional level. It might appear as the biting image of Canadian political cartoonist Michael de Adder presenting the real human disaster at the border crisis and a president's seeming intentional ignorance of the humanitarian crisis (de Adder, 2019) that trended and raised awareness like no factual account could:

*The shocking image of Oscar Alberto Martinez and his
23-month-old daughter Angie Valeria, losing their life
while crossing through the Rio Grande River to get into
the US once again brought the problems of migrants into
a highlight.*

(Team Latestly, 2019)

Or take, for example, the depressing imagery of Banksy's
Dismaland Exhibition (Banksy, 2015) with its almost sinking
dinghies full of refugees painted on grey-brownish walls. Or on a
more positive celebratory moment, the Repainting History Project
of Photographer Horia Manolache, who in detail captured
individual refugee personalities in exact poses and background of
known oil-painted portraitures of European Royals (Gasser Ali,
2019).

And then there is the cleverly put together popular music boy
band The Breunion Boys, with their as cleverly constructed Song
'Britain Come Back' (Breunion Boys, 2019), which is as funny as it
is poignant, evoking in any Remainer that yearning back for a
united Europe. Closer to my home of Stoke-on-Trent, there is the
love of a local home as expressed in the DIY songs of Merrym'n
from Stoke-on-Trent singing about past garden festivals and the
local area (Merrym'n, 2017).

The DIY matters here, as Stoke is one of those left-behind places
where residents and citizens have developed a powerful DIY and
can-do attitude, mixed with a powerful creative talent and a
pragmatic work ethos mixed with a strong community spirit that
has allowed Stoke-on-Trent to become one of the most uniquely
creatively driven post-industrial cities that I have experienced. But it
is also known as Brexit Capital and has some of the most
poverty-stricken neighbourhoods whilst being the regional home of
one of the highest paid CEOs in the United Kingdom running a
global gambling business, arguably feeding gambling addiction
(Neat, 2017). Thus in this city, the same extreme opposing forces
play out in social, economic and political life as they do in the
whole of the United Kingdom.

These tensions and ruptures can only be healed by a more
holistic and empathetic understanding of diverse sets of lives and

their circumstances, and art here is the needed scaffold. Art has the power to move us in ways no facts or rational arguments are able to. Art can touch us and with it affect action in times when the process of normalisation, fear and societal trauma seems to have paralysed us to the point where we seem to allow the most basic human civilities to be undermined. And when we feel the most helpless and consequently are in danger of becoming numbed by some of the acts of barbarisms forced to be endured by our fellow human beings, art is often the way we can communicate and cut through the barriers of partisan divisions to affect change.

Or, formulated in more positive terms than the ones described above, and coming back to my vision for this book that I started a couple of years ago, this book is about the delightful ways of exploring the nooks and crannies of where art finds itself in academia, and how it helps to engage with the outside world to shape our collective futures.

Carola Boehm, pre-pandemic first draft, 04/08/2019
(88 days to the 3rd Brexit deadline)

Carola Boehm, intra-pandemic, second draft, 11/01/2021
(during another lockdown)

Carola Boehm, pandemic recovery, final draft, 06/01/2022

ACKNOWLEDGEMENTS

The idea of a book that attempts to bring together two professional passions of my life, that of arts education and that of the role of universities, has been part of a longer journey within my academic career. There have been so many people along the way who influenced and helped refine my thinking. Formulating new lines of enquiry, bringing together old and established knowledge to uncover new insights, this is never a purely solitary experience. So the list of thanks is almost never-ending. But in a feeble attempt to make my gratitude public, I hereby acknowledge the following communities, individuals and organisations for having enriched my thinking life and thus made the contents of this book possible.

First, I want to thank Staffordshire University, the Leverhulme Trust, the European Union's Erasmus+ and the Arts Council England, who, through their support of my projects, allowed me to explore the role of arts in academia in a research context, an educational context as well as a leadership context. Research, education and leadership are never as separate in practice as they seem in theory, and the combination of these helped crystallise out some of the conceptual boundaries. A big thanks goes to my creative communities, both within the academy and outside of it. During the writing of this book, I was fortunate to be in the midst of various creative initiatives, often close to the region I love and work in, with individuals passionate about the impact that arts can have in everyday life. During this period, we formed a new cultural compact, we initiated a new creative oriented research centre, and we developed new ways of supporting the next generation of brilliant creative and cultural leaders. This was the daily practice in which my own research journey was set, and the resulting knowledge immensely contributed to this book. I also have had the

immense fortune to be part of an academic community that
continually strives to think about and develop our collective university futures, ones that are able to meet the biggest challenges for
humanity. This community is spread across the globe, and their
concern and proactiveness ensure that we have solutions and a
growing mass of underpinning critical frameworks for higher
education. Having spent now almost 10 years in these communities,
I was able to be part of founding a new scholarly society to support
this knowledge production, to provide safe online environments
where international scholars can debate and test out their critical
insights and to learn within the discipline of higher education
studies from so many other academics coming from a variety of
fields, from philosophy, social sciences, educational policy, history
and many more. There are several disciplinary oriented academic
communities that have been immensely influential to me in my
thinking. There is the academic community from which I started
out from in my academic journey, that of music technology.
Interacting with the diversity of academics in this field has continually given me insights into some of the key aspects of academic life
and knowledge production: from how we facilitate interdisciplinarity in higher education to finding solutions to breaching
the gap between theory and practice in our various creative disciplines. Through discussions as part of co-edited books, podcasts,
PhD supervisions and through designing undergraduate learning
environments, this community was my first home and continues to
be at my heart. On a personal level, I thank my family, who have
been patiently supporting my academic endeavours, ones which
needed a lot of teas and coffees. During the writing of this book, all
of us not only directly experienced the biggest humanitarian crisis in
our lifetime, but our children grew up, became adults, landed their
first jobs and managed to find ways to connect in a suddenly,
physically and socially distanced world. I thank my friends and my
social circles for supporting all of the things that create mental,
emotional and physical resilience. Thanks to that support, I not
only finished the book, but like so many during this crisis, I also
became a runner, an indoor rower, a yogi, hitting my first 10k at
the time where I also finished my first rough draft. Last but defi-
nitely not least, I want to thank my ever-so-patient book editors at

Emerald. Writing a book is a big project, and many of us academics working in full-time higher education often struggle to find that down-time to entirely focus on larger projects such as this. I thus particularly thank them for both being patient as well as supportingly keeping this project on track through a time in which we all experienced severe disruptions to our personal, social and professional working lives.

I'd also like to thank the respective publishers who granted permission to present sections from the following publications, all of which I was the lead or sole author for:

Boehm, C., Lilja-Viherlampi, L., Linnossuo, O., McLaughlin, H., Gomez, E., Mercado, E., Martinez, O., Kiveläand, S. and Gibson, J. 2016. Contexts and approaches to multiprofessional working in arts and social care, *Journal of Finnish Universities of Applied Sciences (UAS Journal)*. [Online]. Available at: https://uasjournal.fi/in-english/contexts-and-approaches-to-multiprofessional-working-in-arts-and-social-care/

Boehm, C. 2014. A brittle discipline: Music technology and third culture thinking. In *Proceedings of the Sempre MET2014: Researching Music, Education, Technology: Critical Insights*, Eds E. Himonides and A. King, pp. 51–54. [Online]. International Music Education Research Centre (iMerc), Available at: http://www.sempre.org.uk/conferences/past-sempre-conferences/42-researching-music-technology-in-education

Boehm, C. 2019a. *Environment Trumps Content: University in the Knowledge Society*. Wonkhe. [Online]. Available at: https://wonkhe.com/blogs/what-is-of-value-in-our-universities/ [Accessed October 18, 2019].

Boehm, C. 2019b. *Sustaining University Arts can Give us the Antidote to our Toxic Political Culture*. Wonkhe. [Online]. Available at: https://wonkhe.com/blogs/sustaining-university-arts-can-give-us-the-antidote-to-our-toxic-political-culture/ [Accessed October 18, 2019].

Boehm, C. 2016. Academia in culture 3.0: a crime story of death and rebirth (but also of curation, innovation and sector mash-ups), *REPERTÓRIO: Teatro & Dança*, 19(27), 37–48.

1

INTRODUCTION

Art schools in our universities play a big role in many different ways and not only within the institutions they are situated in. When considering that engaging in arts and culture has a demonstrable but indirect effect on Innovation, Welfare, Social Cohesions, Entrepreneurship, Local Identity and the Knowledge Economy, our universities can and do use arts to make themselves more permeable, to allow knowledge to spill out and be engaged with, to engage and provide co-created spaces of learning. As Sacco (2014b) points out, art and culture are important as it is

> ...not simply a large and important sector of the economy, it is a 'social software' that is badly needed to manage the complexity of contemporary societies and economies in all of its manifold implications.
>
> (Sacco, 2014b)

So this book is timely in exploring where creative practices and arts live in our higher education communities. How do creatives shape this creative education ecosystem? How does art provide an interface between what is within and outside of our knowledge institutions? And why should all of this matter for our communities, the economy and for our society, specifically in a post-pandemic recovery?

And with all that comes the advocacy of providing a strong justification that we need creative provisions in our universities, as there are few more powerful tools left to our disposal that can glue together and heal our divided society and our fragmented humanity. COVID-19 has brought an awareness of the need to think differently, to be bold and not accept that the trajectory of our pre-COVID world needs to be adjusted in order for our species to survive. Our old ways of working, living and playing will not serve our contemporary contexts any longer.

Perhaps exactly because Universities are one of the few sufficiently public-funded institutions left that cover the whole country, they have increasingly been the focus of ministers wanting to turn the last levers to make all of our nation's miseries disappear (Boehm, 2019a). Before the pandemic and during 10 years of Hunger-Game austerity and three years of Brexit-Blindness, Universities were continually and increasingly being asked (some would suggest 'media-shamed') to take responsibility for (1) growing economic productivity; (2) increasing social mobility; (3) solving the challenge of our failing school systems; (4) meeting the increasing expectations of student consumers; (5) reducing immigration and (6) doing all that with decreasing public funding and simultaneously being increasingly forced to allow market forces to regulate their work; because, of course, this has worked so well in other sectors.

Post pandemic, ministers seemingly busy on a day-to-day basis and unable to or unwilling to attend to the more medium to long-term needs of our societies and economies are too often resorting to dog-whistle politics, such as devising cancel-culture related policies (see Williamson, 2021a) that will make it more difficult to de-platform speakers in our universities; as if this was a genuine demonstrable issue or as if we had not just had 18 months of lockdowns refraining our abilities to meet or hear speakers live and in person. And of course, the next threats to Higher Education, announced in the Queen's Speech in 2021, are targeted again against our creative and cultural subject disciplines, displaying them as 'dead-end courses that leave young people with nothing but debt' and announcing a bill that 'will strengthen the ability of the Office for Students to crack down on low-quality courses' (Williamson, 2021a), not bothering to define what that term actually means and continuing on that trajectory of willfully ignoring the economic but also social powerhouses that the creative industries and sectors are in the United Kingdom. The focus is again on truly narrow-minded, outdated and conservative (with a small c) values of science, technical and vocational provision, but again conveniently forgetting that vocational provision is alive and well, although often termed differently with practice-based provision, in the arts. In a past research project, I demonstrated that the difference of these concepts of vocational and practice-based for the creative subjects is meaningless and is more attached to our value systems within our universities than subject matter and content (Boehm, 2014). A whole chapter will deal with these assumptions, and this is needed in order to understand our creative subject matter in the context of content and value systems.

Within this challenging climate, our universities and specialist institutions continue to represent some of the largest art hubs in Europe.

So in this book, I wanted to explore how, in today's super-complex world, our creative learning communities afford their actors to constantly reconsider how disciplines are structured (or unstructured); how creative partnerships between university, industry and society can provide a kind of social glue; and how in Higher Education – through the arts – we can present a new way of learning, a new definition of what new knowledge is, who owns it and how we creatively (co-)create it. It will explore these concepts in relation to fulfilling sustainable visions for truly connected universities that utilise specifically their own creative learning communities for economic growth and social well-being.

Thus, this book will cover how creatively focused public/industry/academia partnership models have been given a new focus within these present-day policy contexts. Some current terms relevant for this debate are 'Culture 3.0' and 'University 3.0'.

1. STRUCTURE OF THE BOOK

This book explores the role that art plays in our Higher Education institutions, evidencing and making a persuasive case for the contributions art provision provides to the ongoing aims of institutions

wanting to make a societal and an economic impact, to be powerhouses and anchor institutions in their regions and to be
demonstrably persuasive in international debates around policy. It
aims to provide a holistic and easily comprehensive picture of the
diverse ways of how art 'works' within the academy and its influence outside. Its content was conceived before COVID-19 afforded
us all to disconnect with our daily physical work and social spaces
whilst affording us to reconnect within a virtual world of work and
leisure. However, this crisis significantly confirmed the importance
that art and culture play in our economic and personal well-being.
This was true before COVID-19 but especially so in a post-COVID-
19 but possibly post-pandemic recovery of economic, societal and
environmental futures.

The COVID-19 crisis has made even clearer how art lives in the
intersections between university, society, industry and government.
However, art subject areas are also inherently one of the most
vulnerable disciplinary areas in the higher education system as their
highly fragmented impacts on the economy and society are less
quantifiable in monetary terms and thus less understood.

COVID-19 represented a significant rupture, and the pandemic
hit the United Kingdom in the middle of writing this book. But this
crisis made it also much more evident how we as humans use arts
and culture to cope in times of change and in times of crises.

Even before the crises, our higher education communities were
undergoing immense changes – locally, regionally and sector-wide.
There was, and still is, a constant need to adapt to the newest policy
initiatives that conceptualise universities as being responsible for
solving a diverse number of socio-economic and well-being
challenges.

Not many monographs look at the institution (academia) and its
organisational structures that facilitate arts in the academy. In this
regard, I am hoping that this book will contribute to opening up
further debate about the importance of arts in academia in its
manifold occurrences and, with this debate, make more explicit the
role that universities play in our creative economies and communities. I would suggest that the book is the first of its kind (since
some key books were published around the abolition of the binary
divide in 1992) to create a holistic view of arts in the academy. It

does this by providing an overview of where art lives in the academy, describing the diversity of interconnected creative activities from within the academy and its connections to communities outside.

Chapter 2 will provide an insight into the methodology used to research, structure and present the contents of the book, introducing the Cultural Political Economy framework as a useful tool to gain insights into lines of enquiry that cross social, political, historical or structural nature. It was first described in associated writings by Sum and Jessop, cohesively in the book *Towards a Cultural Political Economy: Putting Culture in Its Place in Political Economy* (Sum and Jessop, 2013), representing a nuanced and cohesive methodological framework and providing a 'distinctive approach in the social sciences, including policy studies', combining 'critical semiotic analysis and critical political economy' (Jessop, 2009). It grounds its approach in both 'the practical necessities of complexity reduction and the role of meaning-making and structuration in turning unstructured into structured complexity as a basis for 'going on' in the world'. Not only does this chapter thus provide a structural overview of the contents of the book as an adaption of this framework, but I hope it provides an example, a sort of toolkit for others to adapt this methodological framework for their own critical lines of enquiry.

Chapter 3 focuses in detail on one of my two so-called 'lenses', through which I will attempt to look at the phenomena of arts in academia and, through the help of these lenses, gain new insights. Having described the method of using a lens in Chapter 2, as part of using a framework steeped in Cultural Political Economy, Chapter 3 explores in detail the concept of Culture 3.0, as first put forward by Luigi Sacco in 2011 (Sacco, 2011), here applied to the context of arts in higher education. This concept has influenced European cultural, innovation and research frameworks, and close links can be seen with a historically, even earlier movement within the United Kingdom, that of cultural democracy, gaining momentum in this post-pandemic era.

Chapter 4 covers my so-called University 3.0 concept, first coined in a WONKHE blog in 2019 (Boehm, 2019a), covering organisational or systemic aspects of arts in Higher Education within our knowledge economy, including sociological views of institutions and their interactions with knowledge, education and practice, here contextualised within the arts. It is the second of my lenses, and this chapter is the first thorough treatment of this concept, adding a new perspective on the phenomena of higher education and the role of universities.

Chapter 5 is the core of the book, covering different aspects of where art lives in the academy. Using the above phenomenological approach, it provides a critical underpinning, a discussion using the lenses as well as some tableaus, representing something like example case studies that provide a slice in time or subject matter to allow us to reduce the complexity and gain some insights into what we are actually seeing.

In Chapter 5, we cover in subchapters university art schools, art as an academic subject area, the ability of art to make universities more permeable, arts-led research, digital arts, interdisciplinarity, partnership work and aspects relevant to innovation.

Chapter 6, as the concluding chapter, will cover aspects of the COVID-19 crisis. And it should be noted that this book was written in the midst of it and finished during the first signs of recovery. But as the pandemic has proven to hasten many developments or social evolutions, it also has exposed tensions and significant weaknesses for our future creative resilience and well-being. In this chapter, I hope to bring this holistic view of arts in the academy together to map a journey forward and evidence that we are already well on that journey, having demonstrated that not only do we need arts in the academy to stay but also why retaining art in its diversity within our university sectors is so essential.

There are extensive tables provided for future reference in the book, all listed in the List of Tableaus, Policy and other Tables.

This book looks at where art lives in the academia, but with these concepts covered, I am hoping to provide a toolset for academically underpinned advocacy, to hold the slowly but steadily dismantling of our creative and cultural educational underpinnings in our educational institutions, but with a focus here on tertiary education, by demonstrating and evidencing how arts and culture have continually played an important for our economic and societal well-being. In 2021 the Arts Council celebrated its 75th birthday, having its royal charter granted in August 1946. So what could be considered the end of one of the biggest crises in Europe brought about the awareness of how art and culture can heal some of the ruptures in our communities, economy and UK society in general.

With the worldwide COVID-19 epidemic, we faced another rupture that will ripple down the decades, and we can hope that as a society, we and our leaders collectively understand that arts and culture again can bring great healing. Art Schools have become already a significant part of that healing.

2

CONTEXT AND METHODOLOGY

Arts Schools often function as highly effective interfaces between what is within a university and what is outside of its boundaries, and with this, they came to represent some of the largest art hubs in Europe. Art is inherently permeable; it constantly asks for an audience. Its actors live and make a living between being social and business entrepreneurs within a seamless continuum. Thus art, music and performing arts live in the intersections between university, society, industry and government.

Art schools, with their student, staff and professional communities, allow a university to make use of art's inherently permeable nature to create intentional and curated interfaces between what is within a university and what is outside of its boundaries. However, as mentioned above, art subjects seem to also often be one of the most vulnerable disciplinary areas in the higher education system as their highly fragmented impacts on the economy and society are less quantifiable in monetary terms and thus less understood.

Why this is important is that Europe, and specifically Britain, has been struggling with its own pre-pandemic originating productivity puzzle, with the only sector in the United Kingdom emerging victoriously productive being the creative industries (Creative Industries Council, 2017). The pandemic has obviously thrown a spanner into the health of the creative industries, with most of the sectors reliant on live performance having to abruptly stop all of their events which was, for some, the majority of their income.

The Creative Industries had been heralded as one of the few sectors in growth while the productivity of the rest of the economy had stalled; thus, the creative industries were currently outgrowing the UK economy before January 2020.

However, there is also an awareness that in Europe, innovation-led productivity is lagging behind the United States and Asia. As Salmelin (Curley and Salmelin, 2015) pointed out, 'it is important to note that Europe is traditionally stronger in research output and weaker in innovation take-up (i.e., adoption)' and the solution, as integrated in Horizon 2020, the last European Union Research Framework, was generally seen in adopting Open Innovation 2.0 approaches that include quadruple helix partnerships between universities, society, industry and government as well as experimentation, interdisciplinarity, innovation ecosystems and cross-fertilisation. In the United Kingdom, this has found its expression in the 2018 published Industry Strategy (BIS, 2017), including its Creative Industries Sector Deal.

Universities, especially those that are real anchors in their regions (rather than focusing on being competitive actors on an international scale), have a large role to play in allowing new knowledge to drive economic resilience and success. They do this by making use of more holistic creative cultures that include a wide diverse community, including students, staff and a large number of partnerships. The cultural vibrancy that emerges from these partnerships contributes significantly to making a place special, enabling city environments to be attractive to visitors, their interactions supporting community health and well-being through making use of humanity's desire to engage creatively with each other.

It also supports an ever-growing creative economy, providing an enabling environment, both with tangible and intangible assets that directly link to growth in innovation, product start-ups, patents and business growth. In the United Kingdom, all of this has been scoped in a dazzling journey through the UK by Arts Council England's CEO Darren Henley (Henley, 2016).

On the opposite end, there has been a growing understanding of how 'cultural deserts' have had a negative impact on the economy, health and well-being. Where there is insufficient investment in the cultural sector, there tends to be a lack of SME resilience. Luigi Sacco (Sacco, 2014b) links innovation to cultural participation, providing evidence through the comparison of rankings – those from European innovation scoreboards and those from active cultural participation barometers. Simply said, creative and cultural participation is evidenced to build capability for innovation and is strongly linked with innovative systems.

For Sacco, a key issue for Europe is that it is 'hung up' on Culture 1.0 (with a key aspect being gatekeeping and patronage) and that this is holding Europe back in terms of innovation and productivity, as well as health and well-being.

I have suggested before (Boehm, 2016a) that the United Kingdom is 'hung up' on Culture 2.0 (key aspects being gatekeeping, mass production and copyright) with a less but similar negative effect on productivity. Sacco advocates a move towards what he has conceptualised as Culture 3.0, characterised by open platforms, democratic systems, ubiquitously available production tools and individuals constantly shifting and renegotiating their roles between producing and consuming content. For all three concepts, Sacco's Culture 3.0; Samelin's Open Innovation 2.0 and my own University 3.0, art plays a key role in understanding how universities can help resolve parts of the productivity puzzle – specifically for the creative industries which have grown to become such a big part of the UK economy. Various authors have written about university partnerships (Watson, 2011; Etzkowitz, 2008; Carayannis and Campbell, 2012a), but apart from my own publications, art schools have rarely been rigorously considered in this context (Boehm, 2016a, 2017a, 2017b).

The attempt here is to contribute to this area of work, and doing this within a context of current cultural and economic resilience imperatives, necessitating a heightened cultural immersion – what Sacco (2011) has conceptualised as Culture 3.0 – linked to a different kind of university-based learning within a digitally rich knowledge economy – what I have conceptualised under University 3.0 (Boehm, 2019a).

1. CULTURAL POLITICAL ECONOMY (CPE): USING IMAGINARIES, LENSES AND TABLEAUS

In drawing together this book, I needed to make a decision on the methods, the critical frameworks, the terminologies and the worldviews through which the content of this book is conceived. The research underpinning this book used mixed methods and different approaches, both in qualitative and quantitative nature. So for the sake of transparency, a few words about my methodology follow.

Interpretative case studies provide a means to make sense of information which is generally unstructured and of qualitative nature (Mason, 2017), and the focus of this explorative and descriptive content in this book will be on the 'Why' and 'How', drawing from practice (educational and artistic) and scholarly insights (academic expertise, policies and articles) and public discourses (news and media articles). The book will make use of the methodological underpinning frameworks of Cultural Political Economy, as described in associated writings by Sum and Jessop, and cohesively in the book *Towards a Cultural Political Economy: Putting Culture in its Place in Political Economy* (Sum and Jessop, 2013).

This is a nuanced and cohesive methodological framework, providing a 'distinctive approach in the social sciences, including policy studies', combining 'critical semiotic analysis and critical political economy' (Jessop, 2009). It grounds its approach in both 'the practical necessities of complexity reduction and the role of meaning-making and structuration in turning unstructured into structured complexity as a basis for "going on" in the world'. As such, it is what I would denote as an interdisciplinary methodology, or a methodology flexible and complex enough to hold multiple modes of scientific methods, including qualitative and quantitative methods, historical, conceptual or analytical methods, and with this, the founders have called it 'trans-disciplinary' or 'post-disciplinary' (Sum and Jessop, 2013, p. ix and Table 1, p. 13). In brief, they suggest that 'it combines the analysis of sense- and

Table 1. Selectivities in the Cultural Political Economy Framework (CPE).

CPE Selectivity (Sum and Jessop, 2013)	General Examples
Structural (the chosen dominating CPE selectivity)	Considering political interventions in forms of policy, legislation and foundation of institutions. Considering the structure of HE institutions, internally and sector-wide, including organisational aspects of relevant disciplines.
Discursive (supporting structural analysis)	Adding to the above relevant discourse analysis of key policy documents, structured interviews and key discourses of the time. This includes expressions of perceived structures of abstract phenomena, e.g. quadruple helix partnership models.
Agency (supporting the understanding of political-ideological drivers through individual agency)	Considering key agents of political or cultural leadership, including collective local leadership civic society and/or individuals. It can include the voluntary sector, unions and community groups.
Technological (supporting the formation of concepts, such as what are the creative industries)	Considering technological means that have influenced the understanding of related phenomena. 'Technologies shape choices, capacities to act, distribute resources and harms, convey legitimacy through technical rationality and effectivity' (Sum and Jessop, 2013, p. 219).

meaning-making with the analysis of instituted economic and political relations and their social embedding' (Sum and Jessop, 2013, p. 1). As such, it provides a consistent 'integral' analytical method whilst allowing both semiotic and structural approaches, for example, being able to integrate and provide synergy from both discourse and institutional analysis, which both have their places in this methodological framework.

After considering the use of different types of methods, including classical discourse analysis or institutionalism, this method can be considered sufficiently flexible and cohesive to accommodate a study that deals with arts and culture, both in practical and historical terms, as well as conceptual and/or measurement-driven. With the inclusion of more semiotic analysis, it takes account of the 'cultural turn', as understood as a movement beginning in the early 1970s and referring to a shift of emphasis towards meaning and away from positivist epistemology.

It might be worthwhile noting that this 'cultural turn' is a concept different from the 'cultural turn' associated with key policy motivations of the 1990s, which conceptualised that creative and cultural phenomena are accepted and perceived drivers of economic growth. Both methodological and political introduction of the concepts around culture have, however, similar origins in conceptual shifts in the perception that there is a need to understand meaning and culture – beyond language – as part of discovering and constructing digestible slices of aspects of reality. Thus, it is able to bridge anthropological, sociological, economic, political, literary and cultural studies, thus fitting for a study about the role of university-housed arts schools for society and the economy.

The framework additionally provides a structured method to manage complexity by having multi-dimensional means to reduce (or slice) complexity. At present, four modes of selectivity are often applied: structural, discursive (semiotic), technological and agential. With the use of these slicing mechanisms for analysing complex realities, it provides the overarching concept of one or more imaginaries, which 'can be considered as equivalent to the notion of the semantic as a "master" set of signs (signifier, signified, signatum)'" (Sum and Jessop, 2013, p. 164).

How this will allow the subject matter to be considered can be seen in the tables below.

The first (Table 1) provides a description of the selectivities and how they can be used to provide insights into cultural and educational phenomena that have structural, discursive, agential and technological elements.

The second (Table 2) considers these selectivities and provides an example of the application of these to the trajectory of phenomena we are looking at (those related to arts and academia) and which will be explored in more detail in later chapters:

2. MY CPE LENSES

Using the above CPE methodological framework with its imaginaries allows us to use a set of chosen lenses; here denoted as Culture 3.0 and University 3.0 (See Table 3). These lenses are shorthand for a set of trajectories and their evolving meanings and allow us to view accepted and well-known phenomena from a different, estranged perspective. They refer to a whole set of positional concepts that include their own associations to terms, definitions and world views situated in their own evolutionary or developmental trajectories with evolving meanings. They are what in the CPE methodological framework are called 'lenses', allowing us to view an accepted and well-known phenomenon from a different, estranged perspective (Sum and Jessop, 2013).

These lenses are helpful shorthand, but it is important to note that, as such, they will not provide a completely neutral perspective on a phenomenon (and is that ever possible?). Just as using an infrared lens on our night-vision goggles allows us to see an alternative aspect of the same reality we usually see through our eyes, these lenses will force us to reconsider additional aspects of a reality shaped by agreed perceived norms. They make visible a differently enhanced reality. And this should allow us to reconsider aspects anew, more able to be distanced by agreed perceived norms.

The purpose of these lenses is to shift us out of our normally accepted frequency of seeing the world as we are used to and allow us to discover new aspects that may pave a way forward towards a new understanding of the essence of a phenomena, or a novel understanding of needs in relation to actions or policy interventions.

Both Culture 3.0 and University 3.0 re-conceptualise evolutionary or historical trajectories of human cultural engagement on the one hand and the structure, meaning and role of universities on the other. Both together will allow us to see arts in academia through a new set of eyes, so to speak, and with hopefully more clarity.

They are also interlinked and will allow us to see the value of creative provision as interfaces for and within academia.

The emergence of these two conceptual frameworks – Culture 3.0 put forward by Sacco and University 3.0 put forward by myself – can be linked to two interlinked social imperatives of our modern world, e.g. the creative and cultural sectors and the knowledge society. In the case of University 3.0, the curation of new interfaces between communities and knowledge institutions has itself become an important area of concern within UK Higher Education. There is, for instance, a renewed call for public/academia interaction where the engagement with innovation is designed into the research process right from the start. In the case of Culture 3.0, this lens is able to resolve some perceived frictions inherent in the creative sectors, tensions that have their source in seemingly opposing and competing positions of patronised vs commercial art, high-brow vs low-brow art, or private vs publicly funded. This divide is predominantly experienced by policymakers and top-level governance, but much less at an individual level where many (but not all) actors are aware of being able to move very easily between various contexts. This makes economic policy complex, although I would suggest conceptualising creative economic and social activities through Sacco's lens of Culture 1.0–3.0 is able to provide a way forward that might help policy design. Additionally, there has been increasing momentum in, and a public appetite for, process rather than product. Thus the twenty-first century has witnessed a new phenomenon where art (and Culture 3.0) is characterised by the use of open platforms, democratic systems, ubiquitously available production tools and individuals constantly shifting and renegotiating their roles between producing and consuming content.

Why this is important is due to the fact that some policymakers and scholars suggest that Europe is hung up on Culture 1.0, characterised by a distinction between high-brow vs low-brow, arts patronage, gatekeepers and value absorption (Sacco, 2011). I first wrote about Culture 3.0 in articles from 2016, where I wrote about a case study exemplifying the practical implications of Culture 3.0 as part of a university-housed arts centre at a British university (Boehm, 2016a). What became evident then and is important in this section's context is the need for a deeper understanding of the cultural relativity of arts-related practices and the roles that universities play in facilitating various cultural co-produced interfaces between arts and society. I believe these lenses provide a clearer way towards policy design, both in higher education policy as well as cultural and creative sector policies, as they resolve certain tensions (e.g. high-brow vs low-brow, for-profit vs not-for-profit) inherent in a necessarily myopic view of the arts at a particular historic time. With the dissolving of those tensions, they are also able to point the way to institutional policy for designing learning provisions, aiming to ensure our universities are as impactful as they can be.

But furthermore, they make explicit some phenomena in arts and higher education themselves that are worth noting. The lens here itself is worthy of consideration.

Thus the sections in Chapters 3 and 4 are about understanding their conceptual frameworks in order to provide shorthand terms used later when talking about the interactions between arts, culture and higher education as part of a more complex constellation of different dynamics at play, dynamics that include political, societal and cultural developments. The shorthand terms for those lenses are Culture 3.0 and University 3.0.

3. MY CPE TABLEAUS

For describing the case studies in a way that they may have more impact and that they will be able to function in practical terms, I will conceptualise them and frame these as 'tableaus', being made up of a number of 'Gruppenbilder' or 'scenes', most apt to be described as the French term of 'tableau vivants'.

The French term translates as 'living pictures', but it has been made famous by the German Oberammergau Passion plays, which annually provide a festival since the nineteenth century of a theatrical tradition that displays these living images and uses these as a central scenic design (Friedman, 1984). Tableaus are often static or static in the last phases of a scene, usually silent, and typically, attention is paid to the staging and lighting. Often it depicts known paintings but can also depict photography or sculptures ('Passions Spiele' MGG, 1994). And in the contemporary world of Culture 3.0 and a heightened participatory and cultural immersion, this term has echoes of living statues on the streets of our vibrant cities, as well as walking acts in various outdoor and street festivals, which could be seen as a continuation of this creative tradition mixing fine art with performance art, static art with movement art.

Thus, tableaus have a rich history of using the power of art to express messages, be it religious or political in nature. Here in this book, a number of tableaus will depict experience-rich puzzle pieces of a whole, scenes from living case studies, where we can see and understand arts and academia and their impact on the surrounding creative industries and creative communities.

In the context of the key methodology used for this research, e.g. Cultural Political Economy, the tableaus, as listed in Table 2, represent a tightly defined vertically selected phenomena, a kind of vertical slice within an imaginary. I suggest 'vertically' here, as a well-chosen tableau should potentially provide a vertical slice through chosen selectivities; from structural, discursive and agential to possibly technological. It represents a slice in time of a CPE imaginary.

4. HISTORICAL POINTS OF REFERENCE

Using lenses of Culture 3.0 and University 3.0, it becomes clearer how different ideologies predominantly aligned to Culture 1.0 (in the area of visual and fine arts) and Culture 2.0 (in the area of music, media and film) provided challenges in terms of policy-makers' conceptualisations of arts, creative sectors and the role of

Table 2. CPE Imaginaries and Lenses Used Within Arts and Academia.

Era	1951/1953	1980s–1990s	1997–2010	2010	2015 to 2020 (COVID-19)	Pandemic Era
Imaginaries:	Private Cultural Patronage	Public Cultural Patronage	Cool Britannia/ Creative Industries	Austerity Britain	Brexit Britain	Post-Pandemic Recovery
Lenses:	Culture 1.1 and 1.2 Uni 1.0	Culture 1.X Uni 1.0	Culture 2.0 Uni 2.0	Culture 2.0 Uni 2.0	Culture 2.0 (policy) Culture 3.0 (civil society) Uni 2.0 (policy) Uni 3.0 (trajectory)	Culture 3.0
Which crisis:	Post-war trauma	Mass vs Class	Manufacturing	Deficit	Immigration, Europe	Pandemic
Tableaus (see below)	#1 Festival of Britain vs Coronation (1951/1953)	#2 Arts Policy As Cultural Canaries (1965 –1979)	#3 Cool Britannia and the Creative Industries (1997)		#4 A University Housed Arts Centre (2016)	#5 A University Housed Research Centre (2021)

universities within implementing these policies in order to have a specific desired impact.

So some key historic points of reference can exemplify some key trajectories over the last decades of UK developments in arts, culture and higher education. Making use of my lenses of Culture 1.0–3.0, University 3.0 is able to resolve some continuingly perceived frictions inherent in existing political ideologies as well as within the creative sectors and in our society, tensions that have their source in seemingly opposing and competing narratives of private vs public, high-brow vs low-brow culture, access vs elitism, corpus vs content fragmentation, excellence vs access, elevation vs instrumentalism, demand vs supply, individualism vs collectivism.

This divide is predominantly experienced by policymakers, often contextualised in our contemporary politicised world as culture wars, making it harder for the individual to be able to move very easily between the various contexts.

This makes contemporary economic policy complex, although I would suggest conceptualising creative economic and social activities through Sacco's lens of Culture 1.0–3.0 is able to provide a way forward that might actually help policy design, as we will see that it has already helped in some areas.

Additionally, the subject of arts in academia has some additional tensions, between theory and practice, between what is research and what is not. This, in turn, affects how creatively active academics can drive forward innovation. Having said this, it is more usual to consider higher education policies as a separate area of policy, but one, which we will see, has specific implications for creative practices and, therefore, creative sectors.

Again, looking at the emerging policy narrative with a lens of University 3.0, as well as Culture 3.0, will allow the tensions to be seen as a trajectory towards resolving subjective value-judgements of what art is art and what art practices are worthy of research funding, and which are not.

Key policy moments, here using the CPE concept of Imaginaries, can be used to pin this narrative to various time periods or slices to manage the complexity.

I would suggest there are four main phases of policymaking, each expressing a particular ideology of what art and culture are and how they interface with society. They can be perceived as sudden or surprising shifts and dynamics. However, it can be recognised that they are quite logical directions of travel that track a narrative that associates itself far beyond arts and culture. Thus, as we would expect, we see points of departure when political parties come into government aligned with economic or politically motivated ideological conceptualisations of the relationship between society and the state.

Four main periods, or imaginaries, that can be conceptualised as ideological 'packages' are:

- Before 1997 – Cultural Patronage

- 1997 until 2010 – Cool Britannia/Creative Industries

- 2010 until 2020 – Austerity Britain/Brexit Britain

- After 2020 – Post-pandemic Recovery (not covered in this book)

Some of the provided tableaus are brief snapshots from these periods able to present key relevant discourses from that era. A more detailed table of the notable historic events related to an evolution of various policy discourses and aspects of agency is provided for reference, providing a path to where we are today. The terminology and methodology used to explore these cultural shifts are that of Cultural Political Economy, as laid out in Table 4.

Thus with the consideration of the above selectivities and imaginaries, at a top level, we can see a trajectory of the phenomena of arts and academia as laid out in Table 5. These are depicted in much more detail, as a helpful point of reference, in the Appendix.

Table 3. CPE Lenses.

CPE Lenses	
Culture 3.0	Focusses on cultural and arts-related phenomena
University 3.0	Focusses on higher education phenomena

Table 4. CPE and Example Themes for Arts in Academia.

CPE Selectivity (Sum and Jessop, 2013)	General Examples	Examples Explorations for the Topic 'Arts and Academia'
Structural (the chosen dominating CPE selectivity)	Considering political interventions in the forms of policy, legislation and foundation of institutions. Considering the structure of HE institutions, internally and sector-wide, including organisational aspects of relevant disciplines.	History of the Arts Council, NESTA, DCMS, ARHB/AHRC, etc. History of Arts in Education, Arts in Higher Education. History of practice-based PhDs. Emergence of cultural frameworks such as Cities of Culture, EU Culture 2000, etc.
Discursive (supporting structural analysis)	Adding to the above relevant discourse analysis of key policy documents, structured interviews and key discourses of the time. This includes expressions of perceived structures of abstract phenomena, e.g. quadruple helix partnership models.	Public expressions and policy discourses around arts as having utilitarian value/purpose vs arts as a 'moral good'; high-brow/low-brow narratives; the changing understanding of the concepts of arts and culture, creative industries, creative economy; historically shifting or societal differentiated conceptual models to understand the phenomena of arts in society, and creativity in the economy; expressions of artistic communities and disciplines as

Table 4. *(Continued)*

CPE Selectivity (Sum and Jessop, 2013)	General Examples	Examples Explorations for the Topic 'Arts and Academia'
		expressed in narratives and documents of higher education.
Agency (supporting the understanding of political ideological drivers through individual agency)	Considering key agents of political or cultural leadership, including collective local leadership civic society and/or individuals. It can include the voluntary sector, unions and community groups.	Key individual leaders in the political, cultural, creative or educational realm and their impact. Expressions by civil society organisations or industry in relation to the value, worth, structure or perceived essence of arts, culture and creative output. Forming of movements by civil society, creative communities or organisations.
Technological (supporting the formation of concepts, such as what are the creative industries)	Considering technological means that have influenced the understanding of related phenomena.	Mapping and measurement of the creative industries and how they formed an understanding of what the creative industries are and what impact they have on society and economy. Measuring employability or graduate outcomes in relation to the value of creative higher education degrees.

Table 5. Full CPE Framework Used in Arts and Academia.

Era	1951/1953	1980s–1990s	1997–2010	2010	2015 to 2020 (COVID-19)	Pandemic Era
Imaginaries	Private Cultural Patronage	Public Cultural Patronage	Cool Britannia/Creative Industries	Austerity Britain	Brexit Britain	Post-Pandemic Recovery
Lenses: (Sacco/ Boehm)	Culture 1.1 and 1.2 Uni 1.0	Culture 1.X Uni 1.0	Culture 2.0 Uni 2.0	Culture 2.0 Uni 2.0	Culture 2.0 (policy) Culture 3.0 (civil soc) Uni 2.0 (policy) Uni 3.0 (trajectory)	Culture 3.0
Characteristics	High Individualism	High Individualism	Cultural Turn	Corporatocracy?	Co-production Turn	Placemaking
Which crisis	Post-war trauma	Mass vs Class	Manufacturing/ Industry	Deficit/Austerity	Immigration, Europe	Pandemic
Political Goals	Welfare vs Prestige	Education vs Excellence	Economic Productivity	Reducing the state	Exiting EU	Recovery, Levelling Up

Structural	CEMA (Origin of Arts Council 1940). Festival of Britain (1951)	Arts Education in Schools and as part of the National Curriculum	Creative Industry Task Force, DCMS, NESTA, UK Film Council, DfES, Devolvement of ACE to regions, ARHB to AHRC	DCMS, Bonfire of the Quangos. Cuts to public services and arts funding	DCMS shift to digital	Debates about new economic/ social models
Discourses	Art for 'everyone' 'everywhere', 'welfare', Festival of Britain seen as Socialist agenda; Arts as Welfare; Art as an International Pride	1980s and 1990s debate of 'cultural democracy' versus the 'democratisation of culture', e.g. criticism of mass culture vs a defence of intellectual culture; Arts Education in Schools	Definition of 'Creative Industries'; Mapping Document, NESTA Founding Docs, Creative Britain Speeches, Dearing Report, etc. 'Culture and Creativity: The next 10 years' (2007), Creative Britain (2008)	Big Society, 'Philanthropy is good' narrative, DCMS; austerity, cuts to public services including arts and culture	Wealth divides; economic dead ends; environmental unsustainability; Brexit/ Levelling Up	Breaking up of the UK; Pandemic Recovery; Green Recovery; Diversity; Levelling Up; World of work; renewed belief (?) in more state

Table 5. (Continued)

Era	1951/1953	1980s–1990s	1997–2010	2010	2015 to 2020 (COVID-19)	Pandemic Era
Agency	Clement Attlee (Labour); Winston Churchill (Cons) Civil society	Margaret Thatcher and Major (Cons) Civil society	Blair (Lab), Chris Smith (DCMS), Lord Puttnam (Nesta), Tessa Jowell Civil society	Cameron (Cons/ LibDem) Civil society	May, Johnson Civil society	Johnson, Sunak, Devolved Governments, Regions
Tableaus (see below)	#1 Festival of Britain vs Coronation (1951/ 1953)	#2 Arts Policy as Cultural Canaries	#3 Cool Britannia and the Creative Industries (1997)		#4 A University Housed Arts Centre (2016)	#5 A University Housed Research Centre (2021)

3

SACCO'S CULTURE 3.0: A NEW CONCEPTUAL FRAMEWORK FOR CULTURAL DEMOCRACY

Words and terms that have become suddenly fashionable in the last five years are 'co-creation' and 'co-production'. As a recent report notes:

> In considering the practice of Co-Creation (and associated practices) at this time, we must acknowledge that there have been significant shifts in recent years. There has been a move from discourse about the democratisation of culture to more expansive discussions about cultural democracy, specifically in terms of supporting everyone's cultural capability and the substantive freedom to co-create versions of culture.
>
> (Heart of Glass and Battersea Arts Centre, 2021, p. 5)

These terms and their discourses point towards concepts associated with different forms of collaboration. A more nuanced understanding of how we as humans collaborate is emerging, and it includes different forms of working, owning, living and creating as part of a richly diverse set of different types of collaborations that have been part of creative practice in the arts for a long time. Thus artistic research using non-linear knowledge production models or innovation ecosystem models is almost natural, even if those terms are not being used explicitly.

Co-creation, co-ownership and co-production models have also become more important during a time when the divide between the rich and the poor has widened, where power differentials are more keenly felt or as put in the recently published report 'Considering Co-Creation', put together by the Heart of Glass and Battersea Arts Centre in 2021, that there:

> ... is a growing appetite to interrogate notions of power, both in the formation and delivery of projects, but also in the structures we rely upon to support cultural practices. There is a wider demand, in our opinion, for a deeper level of connection and collaboration, and a much broader sense of who gets to be part of the making of meaning, and where that meaning takes form, and how it can affect change, both personal, and at a community and structural level.
>
> (Heart of Glass and Battersea Arts Centre, 2021, p. 5)

This is not necessarily new, but it can be seen as an increasing movement with more and more artists working in this way. In critical art theory, there have been related and long-standing debates around co-authorship and co-ownership, and a line can be traced back even to Barthes seminal 1967 essay 'The Death of the Author' (Engl. version: Barthes, 1977). In one fell swoop or rather one key sentence, Barthes managed to position the concept of an author as a modern invention, one that is intractably linked to the rise of what some have called 'high individualism', or as Barthes suggests, that is produced by the 'prestige of the individual'.

This connectivity to the individual, and thus the focus on the author, is suggested to not allow us to see a piece of work as a text consisting of 'multiple writings, issuing from several cultures and entering into dialogue with each other, into parody, into contestation', and of course for Barthes 'there is one place where this multiplicity is collected, united, and this place is not the author, as we have hitherto said it was, but the reader' (1977).

Beyond the single creator, even in large-scale collaborations of multiple creators, our societies, specifically in the English-speaking worlds, feel as if they are still prioritising the individual above the collective. They seemingly need to emphasise the director, the composer, the conductor or anyone who can be represented as the leader of a collective creative effort, and this still remains a strong instinct within our creative endeavours. Celebrity cultures have increased this tendency even more, and it is not a coincidence that those countries in the western world with the least wealth inequalities have much less of a tendency to foreground, celebrate and promote individuals seen to be the solely responsible creative leaders for what is often a collective effort. It is no coincidence that El Sistema, a music-educational programme that fosters group tuition rather than individual tuition, emerged from the south and is foregrounded as a system for social change (Baker et al., 2016; Booth and Tunstall, 2016), whereas in England during the same decades, school-based and local authority funded music tuition was shrinking, music and arts being cut predominantly in our mainstream schools and local authority provisions whilst private schools became increasingly the places where music was still taught and tuition still provided. As Jonathan Savage so eloquently suggested recently (Savage, 2021, p. 483), 'Government intervention in music education has disempowered music education communities wherever they are located', and this marginalisation of music in English mainstream schools is happening 'despite it being a statutory requirement as part of the National Curriculum' (Bath et al., 2020).

The increasing differentials between the highest earners and the lowest earner in our British society can be seen to also be represented in the creative and cultural space.

So when I have discussed, with Finnish colleagues for instance, the state of the creative sectors in Finland vs England, quite often I hear the response in terms of awe of our English based well-known names of designers or composers, and the suggestion that Finland does not have as many. However, I, as a foreigner, see mainly aspects of 'everyday creativity', and the funding to support this is prevalent with many artists and creatively engaging citizens creating a vibrant environment that is flourishing much more in Finland than in the United Kingdom. The wealth distribution, here, is also a cultural distribution, with – in the average – everyone receiving more arts and culture compared to England, where the average person struggles to access as much and as regularly arts and culture on a daily basis. Thus it could be suggested that wealth distribution has a strong correlation to cultural distribution and, with it, the general well-being of society.

However, more recently and also as a result of our struggles in the United Kingdom with Brexit, COVID-19 and a rising awareness that the 10 years of austerity have simply not worked and were, in fact, an unnecessary intervention that simply increased the wealth inequalities, new thinking can almost be felt to be emerging, one that positions our neo-liberal, unhinged trajectory built upon decades of high individualism as being without sufficient balance with a critical mass of collectivism.

One creative expression of this can be seen in the newest of the Curtis Films published in 2021, all about the tensions between the east and the west as a metaphor for tensions between individualism and collectivism. It is 'a six-part BBC documentary series that "tells the story of how we got to the strange days we are now experiencing. And why both those in power – and we – find it so difficult to move on"' (Curtis, 2021). In the director's own words, 'at its heart is the strange story of what happened when people's inner feelings got mixed up with power in the age of individualism. How the hopes and dreams and uncertainties inside people's minds met the decaying forces of old power in Britain, America, Russia and China. What resulted was a block not just in the society – but also inside our own heads – that stops us imagining anything else than this' (Curtis, 2021).

As Curtis almost hints at but never states outright, we in the neoliberal, marketised world seemed to have associated concepts of individualism with concepts of freedom, forgetting that collective endeavours have also historically secured us the collective freedoms we needed to fight for.

If we see our history of cultural engagement on a linear trajectory, which is fraught with its own dangers of generalisations, we can slowly see a move away from high individualism to a more balanced inclusion of 'collectivistic' approaches or 'co-creation'. Increasingly our creative communities are moving away from 'high individualism' or are, at least, adding more co-creative approaches to the mix. This is also supported by an increased use of digital tools and connectivity that make process collaboration more readily available than ever before. Thus creative clusters and networks, and within these, the cultural artefacts or processes, are increasingly more often than not developed in cooperation, in collaboration and in co-authorship. Often it is not clear who produces and who consumes, when the process starts and when it stops, and what is being produced and what it is exactly.

Culturally conceptualised speaking, this is what Luigi Sacco (2011) calls Culture 3.0, with co-production and multiple author cultures emerging in a time where technological developments make it easy to build new works as collages, assemblages, remixes or patchworks.

Culture 3.0 can be understood as a historical, linear trajectory of cultural engagement, although this simplification does not sufficiently take into account that specifically at this stage of our human evolution, we have all three categories of cultural engagement (Culture 1.0, Culture 2.0, Culture 3.0) existing in multiple layers, and intractably networked into each other.

1. CULTURE 1.0

In Sacco's conceptualisation and historically speaking, *Culture 1.0* was characterised by patronage, and it had limited audiences. Images that immediately conjure up associations fitting this definition are 18th-century flute concerts at the court of Prussia. In fact, I often take the painting of the Flute Concert with Frederick the Great in Sanssouci 1850–1852 at the Prussian Court as a key example. Another image to conjure up what Culture 1.0 means, and one more related to the Potteries in Stoke-on-Trent from where I am writing this book, is a ceramic ornamental Plate made in Stoke-on-Trent, England, in 1855 made by Thomas Kirkby at Minton & Co. Googling those two images will sufficiently provide an image that explains how gatekeeping, limited audiences and patronage are key aspects that characterise Culture 1.0 types of cultural engagement.

Culture 1.0 has gatekeepers where the cultural offering is determined by the patron's tastes and interests. There are no structural, cultural markets or technologies for reproduction. And a key characteristic is that it rather absorbs value than creates it; the money invested in it has to be created somewhere else and from another sector of activity.

But as suggested earlier, although a key characteristic of what was accepted as a cultural engagement in the eighteenth and nineteenth century, Culture 1.0 still exists today and is often the dominant form of cultural engagement that attracts public funding. And this narrow way of thinking about where to invest taxpayers' money can be problematic.

Sacco suggests that 'Europe is hung up on Culture 1.0' and that this is holding us back in terms of innovation and productivity, as well as health and well-being. He links Innovation to cultural participation, providing evidence through the comparison of rankings, those from innovation scoreboards and from active cultural participation barometers (See Table 6).

Creative and cultural participation builds capability for innovation, he suggests, and it is strongly linked with innovation systems, as it questions one's beliefs and world views; promotes acquaintance with, and assigns value to cultural diversity; allows us to experience the transformational impact of new ideas; and builds new expressive and conceptual skills. Cultural participation thus has an indirect but measurable effect on Innovation, Welfare, Social Cohesions, Entrepreneurship, Local Identity and the Knowledge Economy.

However, as we in Europe are (still) hung up on Culture 1.0, and this comes with limited audiences, which in turn – according to Sacco – stifles our innovative potential.

He has an incrementally nuanced model, with Culture 1.2 being set in a time where 'Kultur' is increasingly seen as a component for human development, and public patronage enters the picture, replacing formerly aristocratic patronage. However, the state still often decides on what deserves to be patronised, creating the contemporary divide between high- and low-brow culture. Access to high-brow culture thus becomes a sign of bourgeois distinction or spiritual cultivation. Although there is no substantial industrial organisation, this era also experiences audience expansion, but culture still absorbs value and could be seen as a value distribution from mainly 'citizens who don't attend to those who do'.

Table 6. Link Between Innovation and Cultural Participation.[1]

Ranking Innovation Scoreboard 2008 (UE15)	Ranking Active Cultural Participation Eurobarometer 2007 (UE15)
1. Sweden	1. Sweden
2. Finland	2. Luxembourg
3. Denmark	3. Finland
4. Germane	4. France
5. Netherlands	5. Denmark
6. France	6. Netherlands
7. Austria	7. Belgium
8. United Kingdom	8. Germane
9. Belgium	9. United Kingdom
10. Luxembourg (UE27 average)	10. Austria (UE27 average)
11. Ireland	11. Ireland
12. Spain	12. Italy
13. Italy	13. Spain
14. Portugal	14. Greece
15. Greece	15. Portugal

His model includes different forms of patronage, listing:

Culture 1.0 Classical Patronage
Culture 1.1 Strategic Patronage
Culture 1.2 Public Patronage
Culture 1.3 Committed Patronage
Culture 1.4 Civic Patronage
Culture 1.5 Entrepreneurial Patronage

But the main key characteristic of Culture 1.X is 'patronage', and its geographic centre lies in Europe, where high-brow culture is still felt to need state patronage to survive.

[1]Sacco (2014b).

2. CULTURE 2.0

Culture 2.0 enters the picture with its technological innovations that support mass production, and the high-/low-brow conceptualisation results in the process of commercialisation itself being seen as problematic. A characteristic of this era is unlimited reproducibility of creative content with very large audiences, and this produces significant turnover and profits.

The rise of Culture 2.0 can be seen to be part of the development towards mass urbanisation, the rise of cultural markets and the creative and cultural industries in the twentieth century. The emphasis is on profitability and audience response.

What we have come to know as the Industrial Age, in Culture 2.0 technological innovation also supports mass production, and with large audiences, it produced a significant turnover, making the creative industries the powerful economic sector that it is today. This sector, the creative industries, has often also been called the Copyright or IP Industries, a term that was in the discourse when Labour developed its Creative Industry Strategy in the mid-1990s (See Flew, 2012). After Labour's election in 1997, the 1998 UK Creative Industries Mapping Document even provided a definition for the creative industries as 'those activities which have their origin in individual creativity, skill and talent and which have the potential for wealth and job creation through the generation and exploitation of intellectual property' (DCMS, 2001). As argued by Garnham, 'we can only understand the use and policy impact of the term "creative industries" within the wider context of information society policy. For the use of the term "creative industries", as with related terms such as "copyright industries", "intellectual property industries", "knowledge industries" or "information industries", serves a specific rhetorical purpose within policy discourse' (Garnham, 2005, pp. 15–16).

At the time of the rise of the creative industries in the 1990s and 2000s, these sectors tended to 'double down on the necessity of maintaining high-control copyright regimes, reinforced by technological advances in digital rights management and global advocacy for the maintenance and upgrade of legal enforcements of copyright' (eds. Cunningham and Flew, 2019, p. 5). Flew argues that this was based on the well-established business models of the extraction of rents protected under copyright law but that this has provided limited innovation in areas beyond the usual IP exploitation business models that tended to benefit the IP holders and copyright owners, but not necessarily the content creators (Flew, 2012, p. 20).

This has resulted in the situation that we often see for-profit and not-for-profit creative actors as being on two sides of a conceptual divide, allowing us to understand our cultural engagement only as two very different activities in order for the state to decide where to direct public funding, e.g. what should be publicly funded and what not. And this has exacerbated the high-/low-brow perceptual value divides, with commercialisation to be seen as problematic. Consequently, commercial sectors are often not being considered as of high value to society as those attracting public funding.

But this is gatekeeping in another form, and this simplification has not benefitted understanding of how the creative sector works as a whole, nor how artists and creative professionals as individuals move easily between publicly and privately funded types of activities. It also makes it difficult to understand how we in society engage within and with it, where audiences often do not make a differentiation between commercial or non-commercial participation in arts and culture.

There is also a nuance here that Sacco picks up in his categories of Culture 2.X with (using my own numbering):

Culture 2.0 Mainstream

Culture 2.1 Proto-Industry

Culture 2.2 Counter Mainstream

Culture 2.3 Fan Ecologies

Culture 2.4 Subcultures

The kind of imagery I often use to explain these concepts is that of a Pink Floyd Album, a David Bowie concert or a *Star Wars* poster for mainstream Culture 2.0, representing the key industries driving Culture 2.0: film and music. For the Proto-Industry, I always delight in showing a postcard image of the kilns of the Potteries, placing Stoke-on-Trent's early ceramics industry on the map again, which since the seventeenth century made pottery on an industrial scale. It is a quintessential example of a 'proto-industry' and one that still retains its dominance of ceramic making in the United Kingdom. For Fan Ecologies, I often use the image from our Cartoon and Comic Arts degree at the University, an art-form emerging from – and embedded in – a fan-based commercial world and often considered of lower value, proving the point of the perceived connectivity of patronage with high-/low-brow divides. For subcultures, I use another music album. Released in 1982, the debut punk music album, 'Hear Nothing, See Nothing, Say Nothing', from Stoke-on-Trent's Discharge, has been said to be one of the most influential punk records of all time (MÖRAT, 2016), and punk has proven to be a highly visible and influential subculture built around resisting accepted norms, so very apt for representing something that tried to break new ground. But even breaking with the norm, it still conforms to similar criteria for cultural engagement as do other forms of Culture 2.0.

From the example, it is probably clear that the music industry and the film industry are the key sectors emerging from a Culture 2.0 type of cultural engagement. Key terms describing the main characteristics of Culture 2.0 are 'copyright' and 'IPR', and Sacco suggests its geographic centres to be in the United States with its Film and Music Industries, and I would contend that the United Kingdom represents a centre in its own right with its flourishing Music Industries of that time.

Tableau #1: Festival of Britain vs. the Coronation of Elizabeth II (1951/1953)

An early example of the tensions between what I have above described as Culture 1.0 and Culture 2.0 can be seen during the early years of the Arts Council. And this is our first 'tableau' that allows us to understand how Culture 3.0 conceptual framework can add to our understanding of arts and cultural engagement in society (Tableau #1).

Tableau #1 Festival and Coronation (1951/1953).

Tableau and CPE	Festival of Britain vs The Coronation of Elizabeth II (1951/1953)
Structural Selectivity	• Arts Council • Royal House • Government
Discursive	• Brochures • Newspaper articles • Photographs/Imagery, see Fig. 1–3 • Quotes by key actors
Agency	• Prime Minister Attlee (Labour) • Prime Minister Churchill (Conservative)
Technological	• Technological Innovation as part of exhibitions • Live Broadcast Television

The origin of the Arts Council lies in the period under Conservative-led Churchill Government in 1940, with the newly founded Council for the Encouragement of Music and the Arts (CEMA). During World War II, the CEMA was appointed to 'help promote and maintain British culture'. Chaired by Lord De La Warr, President of the Board of Education, the Council was government-funded and, after the war, was renamed the Arts Council of Great Britain. It was set up by Royal Charter, and by 1945 there were 46 arts organisations funded by the CEMA. The majority of this funding was directed to organisations such as the Royal Opera House and was restricted to Central London.

Although not proven to be correctly attributed, there is a famous quote suggested having been said by Churchill that, when asked to cut arts funding in favour of the war effort, he replied: 'Then what are we fighting for?'.[2] So the initial objective

---

[2]This might have possibly been said by Carter Brown, then Director of National Gallery of Art, in a speech. https://skeptics.stackexchange.com/questions/19143/did-winston-churchill-say-we-should-not-cut-art-funding.

of CEMA was financial assistance to cultural societies finding difficulty in maintaining their activities during the War.[3]

Labour came into government in 1945 and was re-elected to govern in 1950. A project then being very closely associated with Labour was the Festival of Britain. The Festival of Britain was a national exhibition and fair that ultimately reached millions of visitors throughout the United Kingdom. The South Bank site is thought to have attracted 8.5 million paying visitors, with one-third of the British population of 49 million experiencing the Festival in some way (Historic England and Hughes, 2021). Labour cabinet member Herbert Morrison was the prime mover. It included Architecture, Design, The Arts and Science. The political support was divided along party lines, with conservatives viewing the festival suspiciously as 'the advanced guard of socialism' (Hewison, 1995, p. 58) and an unconfirmed but famously repeated quote by Churchill referring to the Festival of Britain as 'three-dimensional Socialist propaganda'.

Fig. 1. Festival of Britain (1951) and the Coronation (1953).[4]

---

[3]The committee was originally funded by £25,000 from the Pilgrim Trust.
[4]Left: Festival of Britain staff outside Lower Campsfield Market. The National Archives, WORK 25/207. Right: Coronation of Queen Elizabeth II, https://upload.wikimedia.org/wikipedia/commons/3/30/Coronation_of_Queen_Elizabeth_II_Couronnement_de_la_Reine_Elizabeth_II.jpg.

An example of the biggest opposing cultural ideologies during this period can possibly be seen in the imagery and the text sources describing the two biggest events happening in the first few years of the 1950s. 1951s Festival of Britain, in its description and its visual representation, was modern, forward-looking, progressive and emphasising its accessibility. The Festival was vast and amorphous and not really centrally controlled (Jones, 2019b, p. 22). The welcoming brochure for the Festival that pinned more than 25 centres scattered across England, Wales, Scotland and Northern Ireland suggests:

> During the Festival Summer from May to September 1951, the visitor to Great Britain will find something of interest going on everywhere.In addition to the centre shown here, cities, towns and villages all over the country will take part in this great national event. With exhibitions, arts festivals, carnival, pageants and sporting events of all kinds, there will be something for everyone to see, to enjoy, and to remember.
>
> (1951 Festival Leaflet)

The images (see Fig.1) were just as suggestive, showing modern women and men in various contemporary clothing marching confidently from the building that boldly had in huge letters: Festival of Britain. The main site featured the largest dome in the world at the time (93 feet, diameter of 265 feet, See Fig. 2), holding exhibitions with themes of discovery, the Polar regions, the sea, the sky and space (Historic UK and Johnson, 2016). But the Festival was almost immediately unfashionable amongst the conservative establishment and viewed with suspicion by political conservatives, despite its clear popularity with visitors and the creative communities. Once the conservative government was elected into power, the site (see Fig. 2) was quickly dismantled.

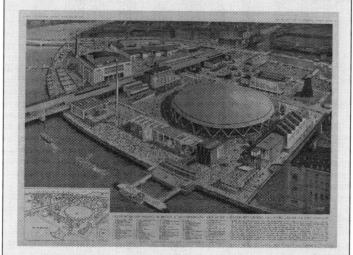

Fig. 2. The Festival of Britain (1951).[5]

This dislike of the festival by political actors on the right, I believe, has very much to do with the definitions and ideologies of concepts of arts, and the thinking of the conservative establishment at that time was very much aligned with cultural engagement being accepted along the lines of Culture 1.0. The Festival was beckoning a more open and progressive kind of thinking of who art and culture was for, and who can participate in it, linked to economic progress that was seen as the key to social progress, and with that, it can be seen as the emergence of Culture 2.0.

[5]Illustrated London News, artist colour drawing by G. Davis, 12 May 1951. *Source*: British Newspaper Archive.

| 1951 The Festival | 1953 The Coronation |

Fig. 3. Contrasting Imagery Between the Festival and the Coronation (1951 vs 1953).[6,7]

Just two years later than the Festival was the coronation of Elizabeth II, now during the time of the Churchill conservative government, and the discourses and visual representations of this event were very much different, associating itself more with history, customs, privilege and exceptionalism (see Fig. 3). The text sources conveyed the weight of history, using terms such as 'investiture of a monarch', choosing traditional places (Westminster Abbey, which since 1066 had been the setting of every coronation), using the Golden State Coach pulled by eight grey gelding horses whose name were listed in many articles, or showing the queen with her coronation maids of honour, all clothed exactly the same but in the dress design is a deference to the more majestic clothing and the 6.5m long velvet trail of the queen's robe.

---

[6]The Festival of Britain emblem, designed by Abram Games, from the cover of the South Bank Exhibition Guide, 1951. The Festival of Britain (1951) (https://commons.wikimedia.org/wiki/File:Festival_of_Britain.JPG).
[7]The Coronation Original Queen Elizabeth II Souvenir Programme Booklet 1953. Depicted is the Canadian version. https://timewasantiques.net/products/coronation-programme-queen-elizabeth-ii-england-1953-programme-for-Canada.

I would argue that these images and the terms used in text sources at the time provide an unconscious and largely non-intentional messaging of who culture was for, who was able to participate in it as an active citizen and who was expected to watch passively in awe.

That the respective prime ministers that watched over both of these cultural events, Labour's Attlee in the case of the Festival and the Conservative's Churchill in the case of the coronation, would have different views on cultural policy is apparent from the imagery and the handling of these two events.

Attlee fully supported the Festival 'for everyone', the deputy prime minister of his government (Herbert Morrison) having proposed it and being put in charge of it. Churchill, on the other hand, referred to the forthcoming Festival of Britain as 'three-dimensional Socialist propaganda' during the run-up to his successful election campaigns. His contempt for the Festival led him to make his first act as Prime Minister in October 1951 an instruction to clear the South Bank site. Even with the key event under his own prime ministership, the coronation, he had a particular view on who should be able to access this cultural event, and he was known to have advised the queen to not televise such a solemn occasion as the coronation (Historic UK and Johnson, 2016).

Considering the element of technology featured in the staging of both events, just the difference of two years made it possible for the Coronation in 1953 to be televised and broadcast to most of the country. As mentioned above, it was actually the future queen herself who – against the advice of Churchill – insisted on broadcasting the coronation, becoming the first major world event being broadcast internationally on television (Castelow, n.d.).

The fact that the coronation was televised, but the festival was not, as in 1951 coverage still needed to be expanded to most of the country (Wikipedia Contributors, 2021a), can be assumed to be a key aspect of the Coronation having a perceived lasting legacy, but the Festival significantly less or perceived as none.

However, within the Festival, technological innovations were showcased, such as the Telecinema, becoming the most popular attraction of the Festival with 458,693 visitors. This later became the National Film Theatre, which in turn became the British Film Institute (Wikipedia Contributors, 2021b).

These two events, using my suggested lenses, depict an ideology of cultural engagement that conforms to the characteristics of Culture 2.0 (The Festival) and Culture 1.0 (The Coronation), and with it come the tensions around what counts as art. This debate is an important one, as often it influences what should be publicly funded and what does not need to be. In simplistic terms, one could suggest that a valid view might be that there are certain forms of cultural engagement that need patronage, as else they would cease to exist. These are Culture 1.0 types of cultural engagement. But Culture 1.0 consequently has the characteristics of being exclusive and having gatekeepers. Any society or any policy drives that are aimed at achieving more access to the arts and using the benefits of arts and cultural engagement for social and economic resilience will need to deal with the processes of making arts and culture more accessible and inclusive, and this is where a balancing of Culture 1.0, 2.0 and 3.0 (as I will describe in the next chapter) has to be considered. But the understanding of culture 3.0 phenomena within the cultural space only emerged in the twenty-first century. In the twentieth century, governments did increasingly realise that arts and cultural policies matter to the electorate, and they increasingly were referenced within election campaigns. There is an increasing mention of cultural policy within manifestos or even as separate, stand-alone expressions of policy intentions.

3. CULTURE 3.0

So then enters *Culture 3.0* with its heavy reliance on digital content production and digital connectivity, albeit cultural engagements fitting the categories of Culture 3.0 do not necessarily need to be technologically imbricated, mediated or distributed. But technology and digital access have made these forms of cultural engagement much more commonplace. Culture 3.0, with its ubiquitously available tools of production, its mass distribution of content happens largely without mediators. One example for this kind of creative engagement is podcasting, designed to be able to be highly distributable, low tech, low effort and resulting in a diversity-rich, high participation rates, with a high audience listenership and low gatekeeping characteristics. Having said this, some Culture 2.0 content producers would very much like to put it back into that box by disentangling it from its underlying technological co-creative abilities to do with its RSS feeds. This struggle over a medium's main technological characteristics being attempted to be pulled back into Culture 2.0 or maintaining its Culture 3.0 progressive and co-creative aspects can be seen in 2019–2022 business deci-sions by company products, such as Spotify podcasts or BBC Sounds. Big companies who have built their income on IP-related ideologies can have real difficulties understanding Culture 3.0 phenomena and how associated new business models might work for them.

The phenomena of Wikipedia is another Culture 3.0 example and demonstrates how these kinds of cultural engagement give rise to or result from open platforms, often with social media sup-porting these. Co-production and co-creation occur at all levels, from ideation, implementation, creation, performance and dissemination.

It is often being seen as 'democratic' with constantly shifting roles of content producers and users. Today, I might listen to a podcast; tomorrow, I am recording one. There is economic and social value produced in sales and participation, and thus it does not absorb value anymore. As it is ubiquitous, it is hard to demarcate the industry. With no pre-determined market channel bottlenecks, the creative and cultural industries in the extreme may cease to exist, with culture no longer an aspect of free time use, but entrenched in the fabric of everyday life. It is immersive.

And as Sacco has suggested that Europe's creative assets and innovation capacity are held back by its Culture 1.0 focused investments, I myself have suggested that the United Kingdom is held back by its primary focus on Culture 2.0 focused investment strategy, as displayed in the last Creative Industry Sector Deal (Boehm, 2019c).

Additionally, the content created through a Culture 3.0 phenomena, often using disruptive technologies, ubiquitously available content and consumer–producer ambiguity, has created new tensions all to do with who owns what and what to do with our gatekeepers (Sacco, 2011). The era of individualism seems to be receding, and co-creation and co-ownership are increasingly taking their place.

Why this is important is that this new conceptualisation can completely bypass the attachment of value judgement to art and cultural engagements, e.g. it simply does not have a high-brow vs low-brow division. It rather sees this as an aspect related to the type of cultural engagement (e.g. 1.0 or 2.0) with particular descriptive criteria. This lack of a more holistic understanding of how we as humans engage in arts and culture has wreaked havoc on our understanding of what art is, what should be funded and how diverse it actually is.

Accepting a high-brow vs low-brow divide leads to exclusivity, as it is based on gatekeeping, as described above in Culture 1.0. However, Culture 3.0 concepts provide a conceptualisation to understand creative and cultural engagement without needing a value judgement or patronage model. Thus the concepts around Culture 3.0 are worthy of being highlighted, as in the absence of this phenomenon of Culture 3.0, authors and creative professionals have often needed to resort to other terms, such as 'community arts', 'socially engaged arts', 'participatory arts' and 'non-traditional arts'. But these terms are often associated with value judgements in themselves. This problem has long since been recognised. Compare Stephenson below:

> *If one accepts a broader definition of 'the arts' then it immediately becomes apparent that large areas of arts activity, especially those centred in youth cultures, are essentially ignored by public sector funding. The discussion can become circular in that young people are often categorised as having little or no interest in the arts, but as Rachel Feldman points out, 'The real problem isn't that young people aren't interested in the arts – many are, with a knowledge and commitment which puts adults to shame … it's just that traditional arts provision has failed to engage their input, enthusiasm and creativity'.*
>
> *(Feldberg in Stephenson et al., 2000, p. 27)*

The scope of these concepts has significant consequences on funding, including who and what can be funded and thus impacting the diversity of what art and culture are counted, which is funded and who has been able to retain a leadership position in these fields. The prospective positive impact, through balancing the Culture 1.0–3.0 ecosystem, makes it important for cultural policy. It has the potential to resolve the long-standing and real struggles for policy trajectories in this field, which go back to the – one might say – formation of the Arts Council (or CEMA) with its original focus on community wellbeing (Hetherington, 2014, p. 105) and ending in a highly charged debate between art activists and the Arts Council, a struggle that seems to wrangle and take ownership of concepts such as 'cultural democracy' (Hadley, 2018; Hadley and Belfiore, 2018; Jeffers, 2017; Duffy, 2019; Arts Professional and Romer, 2018; Wilson et al., 2016; The Movement for Cultural Democracy, 2018; ACE, 2020). There are beneficial implications on how to shift funding to allow more diversity rich and inclusive participation in arts and culture but without the contentious or politicised debates between perceived metropolitan elitism vs democratic access.

Understanding Culture 3.0 can potentially drive new policy intervention by using a new understanding of this cultural phenomenon. Here, the future of an increasing amount of cultural engagement lies in what I would suggest to be a 'co-production turn of the economy', based on the understanding that our organisations develop organically, that we achieve more sustainably for longer when we co-create, that we share in each other's 'acts of creating' and that single ownership of intellectual property is often a method of gatekeeping, rather than a supportive tool of production. This co-production turn of the economy, or Culture 3.0, is a conceptualisation that inherently minimises gatekeeping functionality and embeds a much more fluid access to content production. The Culture 3.0 model focuses on co-production, co-curation and the re-framing of people as both cultural producers and users. In this evolution, power, resources and production are more equitably devolved. Wider society is involved in the co-production of art, so in turn, it better reflects society and its diversity and intersection of identities.

Thus, in summary, the Culture 3.0 conceptualisation, as made explicit in the writing of Boehm and Sacco (Sacco, 2011, 2014a, 2020; Boehm, 2016a, 2017c, 2016b, 2019c), allows for

- Minimisation of gatekeeping functionality, thus allowing minority communities to more easily access leadership positions and funding structures for arts and culture;

- Consideration of 'the diversity and inclusion problem' to be one of definition and eligibility (e.g. gatekeeping and structural exclusionary practices), rather than lack of cultural engagement. Culture 3.0 thus redefines art and cultural engagement to be inclusive of those forms of activities that are already active in minority communities and recognises that the measured lack of diversity in the arts and cultural sectors is one of leadership and funding, but not one of cultural engagement.

- A de-emphasis of the individual, considering a 20th-century concept of high-individualism, and a need for providing an alternative based on collectivism or co-production, reacting to what I have called the 'co-production turn of the economy'.

With a Culture 3.0 engagement in arts and culture, the lack of gatekeeping and the rise of co-creation, there is much less of a problem of access and inclusion. I would thus suggest that what is needed is a rebalancing of our Culture 1.0–3.0 landscape, which currently relies on still public funding and industry strategy heavily relying on Culture 1.0 and 2.0 approaches, but without sufficient understanding of 3.0 to widen to a more diverse access to arts and culture. Culture 3.0 has simply some very society-friendly characteristics, including

- It supports more cultural engagement and participation
- It generally has fewer gatekeepers
- It supports diversity
- It is generally more scalable
- It allows individuals to live more creatively
- It produces both economic and social value
- And with all of the above, it simply has the potential to be more impactful in terms of well-being and health.

Examples for Culture 3.0 can be found in massive online gaming such as the game Destiny, where audiences have started to produce their own media content, being in turn consumed by further sets of audiences. Examples can also be found in podcasting, where local communities have started to pick up the microphones (or just their smartphones) and produce content with, and often useful for, a specific community. Early digital collaborative tools such as Smule's Occarina from 2008 or the Leaf Trombone from 2009 (Wang et al., 2009) were successful attempts of globally socially experienced instrument-based collaboration and co-creation available on smartphones and were able to facilitate instantaneous live concerts involving hundreds of performers throughout the world (Wang et al., 2009). Similarly, the mobile-based Pocket Gamelan orchestra from 2004 (Schiemer et al., 2004), was able to provide instantaneous access to specifically tuned instrumental sounds by using mobiles and I found myself in 2004 twirling mobile phones with the computer music greats of the day, creating an instantaneous churchlike music composition addressing space, performativity and co-creation.

And there are, of course, non-technically mediated Culture 3.0 types of engagements, often found in street festivals and immersive street arts, such as Wild Rumpus's 2017 The Lost Carnival, where audience members found themselves becoming participants within a two-day festival, camping on the grounds and being immersed by stories unfolding around and with them over the duration of the festival. A small example is also the installation of various pianos in various civic spaces, from airports, train stations or outdoor urban parks. One of these I found in Luxembourg, clad in a woollen piano-sized jumper, with the sign 'Music keeps you warm' and inviting any by-passers to sit and play, just for a minute or for an hour.

From a Culture 1.0 perspective, one may ask: 'But is this art?' and 'Who is the composer?' And the nice thing about Culture 3.0 is that these questions do not need to be asked nor answered. What is fact is that individuals sitting down to play are culturally and creatively engaging, and that is what counts. So on the question of whether it is art, I often find myself stating that I can simply say that it is a form of cultural engagement, and with it come all the benefits of any cultural engagement without the drawbacks of having value judgements or gatekeeping access issues.

Culture 3.0 is highly accessible as its key characteristics are co-production and co-creation. Its big emerging geographical centres are, according to Sacco, likely to be in Asia. But as suggested above, here in Europe and beyond, we would do well to make sure our cultural policies (which often still is contextualised in a predominantly Culture 1.0 conceptualisation) and our creative industry strategies (which in the United Kingdom is

contextualised almost solely in a Culture 2.0 conceptualisation)
make full use of this spectrum, from Culture 1.0, Culture 2.0 to
Culture 3.0.

Tableau #2: Arts Policy as Cultural Canaries (1965 and 1978)

Tableau #2. Arts Policy as Cultural Canaries (1965–1979).

Tableau and CPE	Arts Policy as Cultural Canaries (1965, 1978 and the 1980s)
Structural Selectivity	• Arts Policy as part of Free-Market Economic Policy (Conservatives) from 1978 onwards (Beginning of Culture 2.0) • Arts Council 1979 struggle to maintain independence by retrenchment (into Culture 1.0) • New Localism, Mainstream Arts and Cultural Democracy (Beginnings of Culture 3.0)
Discursive	• 1965 Labour Party Policy: A policy for the arts: the first steps • 1978 Conservatives Manifesto • 1978 The Arts, A Way Forward. A Conservative Discussion Paper. • 1979 Arts Council Report (published just before the general election) • 1986 The Culture and Democracy Manifesto
Agency	• Prime Minister Margaret Thatcher • Arts Council • Shelton Trust and Cultural Democracy Movement • New Localism, Mainstream Arts and Cultural Democracy
Technological	Size of the state, economy and the question of the role of taxes, new localism and regulatory governance structures

The 1965 Labour Party Policy 'A policy for the arts: the
first steps' is often quoted as the first effort of a specific policy
dedicated to arts, and the uneasy relationship between the

state and the art sector can be gleamed right in the opening paragraph:

> The relationship between artist and State in a modern democratic community is not easily defined. No one would wish State patronage to dictate taste of in any way restrict the liberty of even the most unorthodox of experimental of artists.
>
> (Labour Party, 1965)

It presented actually similar arguments that Thatcher put forward a few years later, and as she recollected in her memoirs:

> I was not convinced that the state should play Maecenas. Artistic talent – let alone artistic genius – is unplanned, unpredictable, eccentrically individual. Regimented, subsidized, owned and determined by the state, it withers.
>
> (Thatcher, 2012, p. 632)

But the result would be very different. The Labour document continues to suggest that in order to achieve high-quality art and wide availability, 'more generous and discriminating help is urgently needed, locally, regionally, and nationally', exploring civic and art centres as places where the social utility of art can still make more impact.

Keywords of a Culture 1.0 thinking are mentioned, such as 'patronage', 'quality', 'civilised community', but also school engagement, supporting isolated individuals and discussing specifically government support under three headings: education, preservation and patronage. The biggest shift in thinking may be contained in paragraph 77, where it suggests that the responsibility for the arts should be centred in a specific department, one other than the treasury. This was the Minister for the Arts, held initially under Harold Wilson by Jennie Lee, who was also one of the main authors of the Labour Policy document on the arts.

Contrasting this again to 1979 and the years after, here it was made clear that there was no support for public subsidy for the arts in her government, using the same arguments of artistic independence:

> *I wanted to see the private sector raising more money and bringing business acumen and efficiency to bear on the administration of cultural institutions. I wanted to encourage private individuals to give by covenant, not the state to take through taxes.*
>
> *(Thatcher, 2012, p. 632)*

The struggle and the trajectory between who is funding and what should be funded and what not becomes a debate about the value of access to the arts. And this can be seen simply by these two different party manifestos, Labour's 'A Policy for the Arts: The First Steps' from 1965 and Conservatives Manifesto and Discussion Papers from 1978 (CPC, 1978). Just a few years earlier, Margaret Thatcher had, under Labour's Harold Wilson, already tried introducing fees for entry to state museums and galleries, but the policies were rejected in 1974 by the incoming Labour government. Skipping forward to just before the general election in 1979, when the conservatives came into power in 1979 under Margaret Thatcher, we see a policy document from the conservative party, and this recommended that 'that spending on the arts should be protected from across-the-board expenditure cuts and that, when resources become available, there should be the possibility of an increase in expenditure'.

But this increase in expenditure was designed to come from business and individual tax reliefs.

> *We believe that the tax system should give special incentives to individuals and companies to support the arts and other charitable causes. Fiscal changes should be made to increase private support for the arts and these are probably best done within the general law on charities. We suggest that company law should be changed to enable all companies to make contributions to charity. Such donations should be (within limits) deductible for*

> *corporation tax purposes. Gifts by individuals*
> *made out of their income to charities should be*
> *tax deductible. Here again there would clearly*
> *have to be limits and we support the suggestion*
> *that limits should be £500 or 10% of net taxable*
> *income whichever is less. Such a change would*
> *greatly increase the number of supporters of the*
> *arts from moderate income brackets. A further*
> *change which would be beneficial to the arts*
> *would be to reduce the minimum period of dura-*
> *tion for deeds of covenant in favour of charities*
> *from 7 to 3 years to qualify for income tax relief.*
> (CPC, 1978)

Mulholland, in his 2003 book, *The Cultural Devolution* (Mulholland, 2003), describes this as the balance shifting from public to private subsidy, following the International Monetary Fund (IMF) crisis in 1976. This is undoubtedly true. All these patronage systems, state patronage vs private patronage vs public patronage, I would suggest can be contextualised under a Culture 1.0 model of patronage. But the bigger shift comes with the introduction of economic ideology, which influences the perception of the relationship between citizens and the state. The Arts Council at that time picked up this sensitive status quo, and in its annual report and accounts took the opportunity to address – in an insightful and critically rigorous introductory chapter – issues of politics, including the council's status quo as a quango, its relationship to the government and the value of independence from governmental interference in policy or strategy, foregrounding how the 'British way of organising public subsidy for the arts is admired (and envied) throughout the world' (Arts Council, 1979).

Reading between the lines, with the incoming new cabinet, there seems to have been the perception of needing to restate the importance of maintaining the independence of the arts council, described as:

> *...government has put between itself and the*
> *artist an independent body, thus assuring the*
> *arts freedom from political control. Government*
> *pays the piper, but makes no attempt to call the*
> *tune.*
>
>   (Arts Council, 1979)

One can sense the anxiety of losing that independence considering the general election and the Conservative manifesto, promising a restructure of the Arts Council. It mentions explicitly that some politicians had questioned the amount budgeted for arts.

> *A few MPs and peers, wishing to challenge some*
> *particular art activity subsidised by the Council,*
> *have sometimes been frustrated when the Minis-*
> *ter declined to intervene, and complain that this*
> *means the Council is not accountable.*
>
>   (Arts Council, 1979)

Thus, the 1979 annual report stands out and clearly had an audience of the new incoming government to ensure the continued perception of value in order to safeguard the independence of the Arts Council.

That it was successful is clear from the fact that the schemes mentioned were long-lasting; the report details, for instance, the foundation of the English National Opera North in Leeds, which is still running strong today. But that the Arts Council also had a firm focus on high-brow arts, without seeing it as an aspect of potential exclusivity and gatekeeping, can be seen in the following paragraph. This mentions all the key aspects of Culture 1.0 characteristics: being 'high art', demarcating it from 'pop concerts' (which is 'for the masses') and the need for more 'education' in order to widen participation.

> *However, even the most sophisticated marketing*
> *cannot overcome some of the barriers that keep*
> *the majority of the population away from the best*
> *in the arts. These barriers are only partly*

> *financial, since people pay high prices for pop*
> *concerts or a night in one of the many variety*
> *clubs or 'night clubs for the masses' that now*
> *cover the country. The barriers are largely educa-*
> *tional. People feel that the so-called 'high' arts are*
> *not for them, as is shown by innumerable studies*
> *of the audience for the serious arts both in Britain*
> *and America. All depict an audience which is*
> *largely middle-class and highly educated.*
>
> *(Arts Council, 1979)*

This follows with a whole section explaining the emerging practices and concepts of 'Community Arts' but justifying it as a lesser priority by making it clear that with limited and reducing funding, the focus has to be on artistic quality (which from a Culture 3.0 perspective can be defined simply by exclusivity) or otherwise additional funding would have to be found. The predominance and value judgement towards high-brow art are explicit here, but the emerging push against exclusivity and a wider perception of what should be funded obviously created real tensions in the creative communities. This becomes clear in the following section:

> *A recent writer in The Stage, defending the fact*
> *that much community theatre is left-wing, says it*
> *'has had to live with the contradictions of "biting*
> *the hand that feeds", of working to overthrow the*
> *State that enables it to work at all'. It apparently*
> *did not occur to the writer that this paradox*
> *might be harder for the state and the Arts Council*
> *to live with than for community theatre workers.*
>
> *(Arts Council, 1979)*

So in a time when the budgets were expected to be cut, funding for certain types of cultural engagement was easier to cut than others. In this difficult year, it decided to put an end to the activities of the Community Arts Committee and devolve this function to the Regional Arts Associations, and by 1982, the Arts Council had almost entirely ceased funding community arts directly (Bishop, in Bertrand, 2021, p. 5).

> *It has to be confessed that community artists are the most difficult clients for the Arts Council to deal with. It is not easy to work with artists who not only consistently bite the hand that feeds them (a fairly general practice) but often explicitly repudiate the basic premise of the Arts Council's Charter. During the year, a survey of over 40 community arts projects was published, and the author (a community artist herself) makes the following extraordinary statement: 'It must be understood that the so-called cultural heritage which made Europe great – the Bachs and Beethovens, the Shakespeares and Dantes, the Constables and Titians – is no longer communicating anything to the vast majority of Europe's population... It is bourgeois culture and therefore only immediately meaningful to that group. The great artistic deception of the twentieth century has been to insist to all people that this was their culture. The Arts Council of Great Britain was established on this premise'.*
>
> *(Arts Council, 1979, p. 10)*

Cutting national funding meant that the responsibility for community arts types of cultural engagement was placed again with local authorities and the Regional Arts Association. As Bertrand, in a recent article states: 'It deprived the community arts movement from a national recognition and framework and played a role in its future fragmentation' (Bertrand, 2021, p. 6). This systematic remaking or shrinking of the state is what Martin Jones, in his book *Cities and Regions in Crisis*, names as a 'new localisms', wherein 'a process of centrally orchestrated localism certain functions were devolved from the nation state downwards and delivered through an increasingly complex suite of flanking territorial alliances. New institutions were created to bypass the perceived bureaucratic modes of intervention associated with locally embedded and scale-dependent structures of local government' (Jones, 2019a, p. 60). Control was exerted centrally by introducing a high number of regulatory frameworks, such as in education or centrally oriented contractual arrangements (governance) that potentially brought organisations in conflict with the local government (p. 37).

But it also had the other effect that it allowed local and regional authorities to be the main actors in the next chapter of culture-led regeneration, which used community arts and participatory types of cultural engagement for social well-being, and it increasingly informed local policy. Whilst at the national level, the Conservatives had just been elected and began to put through educational and cultural policies with wide-ranging consequences, there was a parallel trend towards the election of Labour councils in various UK cities. These often were committed to favouring participatory democracy and local solutions over the dominant consensus favouring centrally delivered solutions and national economic planning (Gyford, 1985 in Flew, 2012, p. 15), which was existent in both current Labour and Conservative ideologies. The cultural policies of the left-wing Greater London Council in the early 1980s are often cited as a seminal moment (see Hesmondhalgh and Pratt, 2005, p. 4).[8] As McGuigan writes

> This policy thinking was directed against elitist and idealist notions of art, but was also a challenge even to those left-of-centre activists and policymakers who had concentrated on expanding the field of arts subsidy to include new groups.

[8]There were significant precedents at the international level, in discussions of the cultural industries as part of the UNESCO (see UNESCO, 1982 in Mcguigan, 2004, p.175), but these had no direct impact on national and urban policy in the advanced industrial countries. For a fuller account of the Greater London Council moment, and its relation to leftist thinking about cultural policy, see Hesmondhalgh et al. (2015, pp. 22–23) and (Mcguigan, 2004, p. 175).

> *Instead, it was argued by some associated with the GLC, cultural policy should take full account of the fact that most people's cultural tastes and practices were shaped by commercial forms of culture and by publicly funded media such as public service broadcasting. The motive behind this perspective was not to celebrate commercial production, but rather to incorporate a recognition of its centrality in modern culture into cultural policy.*
>
> *(Mcguigan, 2004, p. 178)*

Beyond the Conservative–Labour divide of their respective ideologies that so clearly affected how arts were expected to be funded and what art should be funded, this debate depicts the emerging tensions of a normative culture of patronage (Culture 1.0) moving to something different.

The vision of a more commercially or private funded investment for the arts of Thatcher's neo-liberal trajectory, depicting capitalist individualism, competitive entrepreneurial markets, represented a shift towards Culture 2.0, whilst the Arts Council's report seemed to – as a solution to the imminent problem of budget cuts – entrenched itself into Culture 1.0, funding only the small elite organisations that could provide the confidence of what the Arts Council perceived to be the highest excellence of arts. It was this entrenchment into Culture 1.0 that, from an Arts Council perspective, allowed it to maintain and secure sufficient independence from a hostile government set on reducing its resources.

All the characteristics of Culture 1.0 can be recognised in the Arts Council's expression of its strategy and its resulting impact: patronage, limited audiences, gatekeeping functions (through the arts council itself), high-brow vs low-brow divides, less availability of structural, cultural markets and value absorption, e.g. the money invested in it had to be created somewhere else. For the Arts Council at that time, public patronage was the norm for this kind of culture, and exclusivity was perceived to be a result of a lack of education and theoretically able to be resolved with education, not taking into account the lack of diversity of cultural engagements that this portfolio would exhibit, and with it a lack of accessibility.

This, in turn, was debated specifically in community arts engaging artist communities, whose funding and with it their role in supporting communities through creative and cultural activities had been severely undermined.

New movements popped up as resistance. The Shelton Trust, an organisation of community artists in the midlands, was founded in 1979. A conference hosted by members of this group aimed to discuss new cultural alliances able to set the stage for political and social change. A Culture and Democracy Manifesto was published in 1986, which defined, conceptualised and rigorously put forward for the first time the term 'cultural democracy', suggesting that 'in a genuine democracy people make their culture rather than have it made for them – locally, nationally and internationally' (Kelly & Shelton Trust for Community Arts, 1986, p. 39). This can be recognised as the beginnings of a movement towards cultural engagement that conforms to Sacco's Culture 3.0, considering that Sacco, in the development of his concepts, would have, in turn, drawn from the cultural democracy movement.

And this type of Culture 3.0 momentum puts forward resistance to Thatcher's cultural-oriented economics, which could be mapped to the beginnings of Culture 2.0, as well as the Arts Council's retrenchment into elite, prestigious art for the few, more aligned to the normative Culture 1.0.

The tensions are there in the discourses of the day, already exhibiting the trajectory from one type of cultural engagement to another and moving towards a third.

4

UNIVERSITY 3.0: A CONCEPTUAL FRAMEWORK FOR REVISITING UNIVERSITY FUTURES

Turning to our higher education (HE) sectors, there is a general acknowledgement within our university sectors that there is a shift already beginning to emerge in how our HE institutions facilitate learning within their learning communities. So to understand this trajectory over the last 2 to 3 decades and to be able to imagine a university future that is able to adapt to contemporary challenges on structural, pedagogical, technological and social levels, I have started (Boehm, 2019a) to use a conceptualisation of an evolutionary journey from University 1.0 to University 3.0.

1. UNIVERSITY 1.0

In this conceptualisation, *University 1.0* represents more predominantly those periods and institutional cultures associated with an inherent perception of 'knowledge ownership', including, for instance, modern aspects of institutionally owned IP and copyright. This 'knowledge patronage' model influences how content is managed, taught, protected and produced. Typical teaching practices include processes that represent a knowledge exchange from those employed within the institution to those who don't (such as large lectures).

And the cultural shift from University 1.0 to 3.0 has happened in my lifetime. My first academic substantive lecturing post started in 1997, and I progressed from my post to another university only in 2007. When embarking on an academic career as a lecturer in music technology, in these first 10 years, I was teaching acoustics and music technology subjects in the classical model of lecture plus practical. I would give a lecture on the subject, informed by expertise and my predecessor's expertise, and then we would embed that knowledge through practical sessions that usually entailed smaller classes.

But during these 10 years, our society moved into a knowledge society. Wikipedia launched only in 2001, and I remember the first half-decade of its existence, the repeated mistrust of the academic communities in a collectively edited, seemingly unauthorised canon of knowledge. The iPhone only came out in 2007, only then bringing your knowledge into your pocket. Until then, I – as the lecturer on acoustics – was the key authority to allowing the exchange of knowledge to happen from me to learners. I represented the key resource from which learners derived their knowledge. And although even at that time, I annually stressed to first-year students that we, the lecturers, were only one of many resources at the fingertips of students during their time at our university, we were not yet living in a knowledge society, although we were involved in building it.

It still seems almost unbelievable, as I, for one, do not consider myself ancient, but I went to the third ever World Wide Web Conference in Darmstadt in 1995. I understood the power of the internet to come, the significance of metadata, search algorithms and the futuristic concepts from that time of a future where music would come from a tap, just like our electricity. And my own academic journey led me to work in this field, being involved in those first 10 years in music mark-up languages, metadata, mpeg7 and music information management systems for time-based media.

But when lecturing about digital audio, dithering, the cochlea, room acoustics or Helmholtz resonators, the difference to now was that then no student could quickly pull out their smartphone and look up on Wikipedia what all these terms actually meant. The almost sole source of knowledge was me and the university library.

And that is why lectures are often deemed to be such an ancient way of conveying knowledge in our modern HE systems, as learners of today rather live and breathe knowledge around them. It is at their fingertips, and that is why we need to and have changed our pedagogies substantially from that time. Having said that, I have to admit that I like a good lecture, and I think the critics of classical lectures also often forget to consider the psychology of the humbling experience of a learned individual speaking at the front of 600 students engaging in that collective act of listening intently. This experience demarcates us from schools and colleges as well, and the process in itself shifts a learner's attitude toward knowledge, listening, collective experiences and developing a specific relationship with a learned individual. Include some interactivity and group work in lectures, and I think this University 1.0 pedagogics can still be transformed into a valuable learning experience in a University 3.0 immersed student community.

2. UNIVERSITY 2.0

University 2.0 moved into the era of massification of HE, characterised by expanding and fragmenting knowledge domains (Boehm, 2014) and the use of metrics to personalise mass-produced and marketed learner products. Like a box of assorted chocolates, we were able to personalise through learner analytics to the extent that learners felt they received what they needed whilst experiencing a 'mass-produced' service. We see the emergence of quality assurance products (e.g. validations), standardisation of content (e.g. QAA benchmark statements) and concepts around students as consumers and universities as businesses. But a key aspect remains – that knowledge is central.

We academics were (and still are) curating the knowledge for our learners as we navigated these fragmented fields of content, the fragmentation of knowledge resulting from expanding knowledge fields. That is to say that knowledge had become expanded to such an extent that deep knowledge domains increasingly appeared as unconnected fragments within larger subject areas. This fragmentation is what Sperber (Sperber, 2005) re-conceptualised as 'brittleness' and consideration of how to connect these domains took on a new momentum with an increase of scholarly work and practices into interdisciplinarity in HE.

With this fragmentation comes the debate of value, e.g. University 2.0 conceptual models have an inherent friction between knowledge depth and knowledge breadth; between the transactional purpose of knowledge/skills vs the basic need of humans to pursue a better understanding of our role in the world. And this tension also feeds into the debates around low-value courses that are currently in 2022 still raging and creating a lot of existential angst in various VC offices. These debates are framed in a context of quality and value (DfE & Hinds, 2019; O'Brien et al., 2019), of 'driving up standards' and that 'in this new era of choice students don't have to settle for poor value' and 'quality' (DfE & Williamson, 2021). This debate also feels like a dog whistle for an electorate which is evidenced to be generally less urban and less educated, rather than a debate on how we, as a society, can sustainably fund our universities. And of course, it completely ignores the fact that, once having set universities on their path of embracing private market ideology, with universities competing for their students, with student fees paying substantially for their own tuition, with a degree becoming a choice of the individual rather than an offer to society as a whole, university's biggest sustainability criteria is student demand. And this student demand is often not in areas that might be perceived to be needed for our future society to function economically and structurally. So cutting popular humanities and arts courses within this kind of thinking should result in more engineering and technical courses, but the incentives needed to put into the system to balance this is more difficult than the original student number targets, which were able to be controlled much more steadily and centrally.

Thus University 2.0 models have the same tensions that all neo-liberal associated economic systems have; they are divisive and exaggerate inequalities. Thus many post-92 universities, aptly denoted as recruiting universities, struggle with the annual fluctuations of student income and have to spend a substantial proportion on marketing, whilst the older traditional universities, denoted as selecting universities, still benefit from a prestige based market and a biased research funding system that allows them to have more diverse income streams, from research, teaching, international students and enterprise initiatives, and without having to invest as much into marketing, nor their physical infrastructure to attract learners.

Simon Marginson said in 2014 that there is still no such thing as a HE market, that commerce is marginal to the sector. The 'higher education market' simply does not exist as if 'Oxford and Cambridge increased market share, they would reduce the exclusivity and value of their degrees'. This refers to the long misunderstood prestige market that existed in HE and in our University 2.0 systems. And in this 'market', 'consumer power cannot truly govern selective universities. They remain producer controlled. As the disgruntled consumer walks out of the door, she or he passes a queue of others waiting to enter. (…) Genuine customer focus takes root only among lower-status providers with unfilled places' (Walton, 2014).

But this does not mean that various governments of the day are not still trying with all their efforts to push this unwieldy sector, which Watson rather likened to 'turbulent Italian Renaissance Towns' (Aitken in Watson, 2009, p. 85), into some guise of neoliberal markets.

Over the years, recent governments have introduced various forms of market competition into the HE sector, 'deregulation' and 'freedom' to innovate, but on the other hand, it simultaneously asked for the highest amount of scrutiny. It has incorporated a centrally controlled and public accountability that few private sectors experience (Rushforth, 2017). I am possibly being slightly overdramatic, but I have often seen this as English universities being torn asunder, on the one hand, asked to act like businesses, while, on the other, having to undergo intense public-accountability processes. From my perspective, this felt like being knotted tightly into a public accountability straitjacket, with hands and feet tied behind your back, whilst having been thrown into a competitive free market shark tank. The only movement left was squirming defensively, and that is certainly what the HE sector has been doing over the past decade.

The tensions can also be understood when considering HE sectors in a neo-liberal contextualised market economy, as Roger Brown has done in his 2013 analysis: *Everything for Sale? The Marketisation of UK Higher Education* (Brown and Carasso, 2013).

Neo-liberal conceptualised market economies, unlike Keynesianism, focus on the supply side. Thus quality assurance processes have been afforded to increasingly focus on content as product, in order to be able to 'package up' learning. I would suggest the widespread use of Bloom and his Taxonomy did not help in understanding some of the tensions in this process but rather ended up being used to support a structured approach for this act of packaging up learning content.

Quality assurance processes themselves have been packaged up as products. Conceptualised as another product rather than a process inherently attached to a learning community of practice, validation products thus emerged predominantly out of those HE sectors that had strong University 2.0 (or marketised HE systems) at its heart. It is no coincidence that one will find fewer German or Finnish Universities validating international, Asian or Indian degrees, as the progression into neoliberalised higher-education frameworks is much less advanced.

The way validation is structured in the Anglo-American, neo-liberal university frameworks also provide insights into this University 2.0 way of thinking. Here we often find the assumption that one can validate the content separate from delivery, as many English-speaking universities do with their validated partner provisions being quality assured in its delivery only, with the content being approved in separate processes.

However, I am not convinced that we have improved our learning environments and achieved more learned graduates when separating the delivery from the content. So much of human nature, of constructive learning, of group and peer learning dynamics seem to be not taken into account in this separation.

Brown defines 'Marketisation as the attempt to put the provision of higher education on a market basis, where the demand and supply of student education, academic research and other university activities are balanced through the price mechanism' (Brown, 2015). As Brown contends, 'Through marketisation neoliberalism is having the same effect on Higher Education as it has on society generally, particular on the provision of Higher Education, e.g. supply and organization of the sector' (Brown, 2018). Devising a list and expanding from a 2018 talk by Roger Brown on Neoliberalism, Marketisation and Higher Education, the neo-liberal conceptualisation of the University sector in its fallacy should become more transparent (see Table 7).

But neoliberalism, and with it, my own University 2.0 concept, is not a coherent set of policies. So although the current Department for Education is attempting to bring about a market by an intensification of a regulatory regime, it is also useful to disentangle from other current trajectories, such as globalisation, financialisation and digitalisation. Having said this, neo-liberal conceptualisations have certainly accentuated this momentum to the detriment of the potential benefits, and as Brown lists, it has:

- Weakened financial markets,
- Weakened the benefits of globalised trades,
- Failed to enable workers to adjust to technologically markets.

This focus on product and marketisation, and with it an emphasis on the individual, including personalisation of a mass product and service, has resulted, according to Brown, in:

- University campuses looking like shopping malls
- VCs increasingly becoming CEOs
- Universities being reinvented as PLCs (Public Liability Companies)
- Governing councils become company boards
- Educational departments becoming income generating units
- Staff assessed in relation to the bottom line
- And, of course, students having to be recontextualised as investors and consumers, ones that take out loans.

Table 7. Effects of Neo-Liberal Economic Conceptualization on the University Sector (see Brown, 2018).

Neoliberal Policy Model in General	UK Higher Education Specifically
• *Deregulation*: Abolition of barriers to free movement of goods, people, services. Business should be able to get on with the minimum of red tape. • *Privatisation* (because this is perceived to be more efficient, and competition is perceived to lift quality under neo-liberal thinking). Tax reduction and *shrinking of the public good*: state funding should be reduced to focus on core functions such as security, defence, justice. • *Trickledown economics*: Wealth gained through these savings should trickle down to society. This is increasingly understood to simply not work. • Welfare programmes should only be at *basic level of security*, this should incentivise work. • *Focus on Supply*: Macroeconomic policy should be about reducing inflation. Main barrier to growth is on the supply side. Governments should not influence demand. Thus reduce power of unions, austerity is a continuation of this.	• *Deregulation*: Removed barriers for new for-profit entrants. Introduced market forces in HE. • *Privatisation*: Reduced public funding through student loan system. Allowing for-profit HEIs. • *Trickledown economics*: Binary divide is still stark, although slowly decreasing. However, casualisation of staff, fractionality, mobile workforce, insecurity, instability is increasing. • *Staff morale*: Hire-fire cultures in HE. Staff assessed in relation to the bottom line. Departments becoming income generation units. • *Focus on Supply*: Emphasis is on the supply side: product/service focussed rather than socially constructed negotiations of values within communities of practice

The justification for these neo-liberal introductions into our market economies was growth, investment, lower unemployment, productivity, innovation and debt. But the biggest irony is that neoliberal ideologies have been evidenced to fail on almost every level. It has led to inequality, child poverty, insecurity, massive transferal of wealth from the majority of the population to the small top per cent and unfair distribution of power, including political power and electoral power.

This stratification in society is mirrored in University 2.0 sectors, which display similar failings, opposite to government's claims of the benefits of increased competition. Brown (Brown, 2010, pp. 6–19; 2017, 2018) lists the following headers, expanded by my contextualisation within a University 2.0 model:

1. Increased stratification between the highest earners and the lowest earners within a university, as well as the richest and the most financially vulnerable universities in the UK HE sector as a whole. It is often not recognised that the reason the sector has a prestige-based market, is that comparison between institutions is too complex, despite all regulatory interventions. This diversity is something I hope we can celebrate at some point, rather than find the next aspect of HE to put into a regulatory straight jacket and argue with the concept consistency, whilst mistaking it for conformity. Increased stratification is also a real issue, with four members of the Russel Group owning 60% of assets (HESA statistics from 2011, in Brown, 2018).

2. We have also seen a reduction of diversity in the HE sectors through externalising strategy, being afforded to attend to per-formance metrics set external to the institution. This resulting isomorphism is a consequence of regulatory frameworks and the extensive use of externally set league tables used as internal quality indicators. The almost complete adherence to league tables devised by individual outlets devising their own algorithm (and adapting it to fit a status quo) without much resistance seems so absurd to me and can only be understood as herd behaviour on a sector level. And I do wonder when this will break, and universities will start to reject the externalisation of their strategic priorities by hunting after these external measures. Additionally, the government suggests it desires a diverse,

innovative sector with individual institutions having their own USPs, whilst putting in regulatory frameworks and generic benchmarks that all HE providers will have to try to meet.

3. There is certainly less and less innovation as we have seen the powers of OfS increase, and with it, various existential risks. The current set-up of OfS leads institutions to play safe, and not verve too far from the mainstream.

4. Increased risk to quality, with for-profit alternative providers having inbuilt conflicts of interest with their shareholders (which, in my experience, is not as detrimental to the student experience, as it can be for working standards of staff employed by these institutions). And as students begin to see their education as a service they have paid for, and naturally feel a right to achieve a degree, we see increases in cheating and essay mills. The stakes are higher now and more fallen as a burden on the individual, and with it, the temptation to minimise the risk.

5. Diversion of resources is pooled to non-core activities, such as marketing. And this also falls unevenly to the sector, with selecting universities needing usually less manpower or involvement of academics, whereas recruiting universities often organising a high number of recruiting events with more of the burden and responsibility of recruitment falling on individual academic departments. It is interesting to note that within Europe, the United Kingdom has one of the highest proportions of professional staff costs vs academics, fluctuating yearly between 51% and 55%. This is also a result of our governmental interference in the autonomy of our universities. We have now one of the most expensive university sectors in the world, and this is a result of a University 2.0 conceptualisation.

6. More than ever before, we have greater instability and short-termism, and this is within a sector that badly needs to consider itself a long-term business, including being able to assess and act on the long-term educational needs of our societies.

7. What has been often rehearsed is the weakening of universities' role in society. Marketisation has posed a direct threat to our universities being an independent source of information for and of society, weakening of HE positions in society, with many universities on top-tier global rankings struggling to be also impactful in their cities and regions. This is a logical outcome; the more that a university sees itself in a global pecking order, the more it will try to reach those metrics that keep them there. In addition, the less our universities are seen as a public good, the less trust they will be given by their surrounding regional communities. A movement that is positive in this regard is the forming of a sector campaign for a civic university mission (UPP Foundation, 2018). Additionally, there is an increase of literature that debates this issue, hopefully providing that critical underpinning on which we can build our future University 3.0 types of universities, trusted by our communities and that are there for a public service (Hazelkorn, 2016; Millward (OfS), 2019; Walker, 2018; Watson, 2011).

Apart from the above, in our Universities 2.0, there are still the concepts of universities being patrons of knowledge, but now being the curators of knowledge for both transactional utilitarian purposes as well as expanding our understanding of reality. But the focus is on a packageable learning provision that has products and objects rather than focusing on processes and environments of learning.

So what to do, and how to move into the next phase of our sectors, the Universities 3.0 of the future. According to Brown (2018), his simple list should probably be on every Vice Chancellor's desk, and I have merged it with my own:

1. Resist marketisation in HE; it does not work. Demonstrate costs and detriments of continuing marketisation. Use the evidence we have to expose the fallacies of the claims made for the application of market theory to every sphere of human activity. It might work when selling socks, but it does not in HE.

2. Refuse league tables and develop your own performance metrics to support your own unique institution's progress into the future.

3. Explain in publicly accessible language what the problems are to your public.

4. Show how to use resources to the best for our students. Remind everyone and often what HE is for, and how it differs from the business sectors and why it should be a protected place for society.

5. Find ways to limit expenditures on marketing and branding, work with the whole sector to agree on limits on market expenditures.

6. Avoid a mode of governance and resource allocation that mirror the worst sides of the corporate sector.

7. And then point out the obvious detriments that University 2.0 models have had, from high levels of student debt, high level of stratification of university staff income levels and job security, casualisation of academic staff and – so far – the opposite of lifelong learning.

8. Support the sector leadership to speak up. It is telling of the fear within the sector and its individualised, but collectively shared experience of existential Angst that, as Brown suggested in 2018, 'collective VCs have been far more vocal on the threats to their research funds than they have on the existential threat to Europe's security and integrity' as fallout from Brexit.

I reiterate that which many researchers have evidenced (Including Brown, 2015; Brown, 2018; Hazelkorn, 2016; Wright and Shore, 2017; Levin and Greenwood, 2016a). The neo-liberal fantasies of a University 2.0 marketised HE system has been a disaster in those countries where it has been taken the furthest. It has resulted in stratification and homogenisation, leaving (ironically) less choice and poorer value for money for both society and students. Our universities have a key role to play to expose the fallacies on which neoliberalism is based, and work with other groups to rebuild civil society.

And specifically for us academics, we need to build up a body of work of conceptual and critical frameworks and pieces of evidence with which we can underpin the next phase of our HE evolution. University 3.0 concepts will be part of this process.

3. UNIVERSITY 3.0

Having covered in length where most of our policy ideologies are in relation to University 2.0, I would suggest that many professional and academic staff already feel that we are now entering an era of *University 3.0* (see Table 8), without being able to label it as such. This is often not well understood by current policymakers, who seem to still have an image of the university from the time they received their degree 30–40 years ago. A short description of the trajectory of University 1.0 to University 3.0 can be seen in Table 8.

University education is becoming more a process of curation of interfaces between knowledge and society; i.e. the quality of a learning environment is becoming more important than specified and static learning content. HE providers are becoming more permeable and learners and researchers more often co-own, co-produce and co-create.

Table 8. University 1.0–3.0.

University 1.0

- Owners of knowledge
- Focus on knowledge

Universities 2.0

- Curators of the knowledge, teachers and researchers as professions
- Mass higher education, mass products
- QAA products, standardisation, student as consumers, CMA, etc
- Linear research to commercialisation routes

Universities 3.0

- Facilitators of learning
- Curators of interfaces between knowledge and society
- Developers of environments where learning happens

There is a big role here for knowledgeable and expertise-rich actors as lecturers and professors, but their predominant role of interacting with learners moves away from transmitting knowledge (University 1.0), and also away from curating knowledge (University 2.0) to facilitating learners to bring knowledge that is all around them to the learning process and managing this complexity in a curated learning environment in which sense-making and knowledge creation is constantly part of that environment (University 3.0). However, current underpinning quality assurance frameworks often comprehensively do not take this into consideration.

In University 3.0, we carefully position various interfaces between different levels of learners, different types of communities and different disciplines. This careful positioning is a process of curating interfaces, with the *facilitation* of learning being at the heart of this process rather than the acquisition of specific knowledge content itself.

This, of course, stands in tension with University 2.0 boundaries due to a larger focus on content-based regulatory constraints (e.g. QAA subject benchmark statements) combined with risk-rich, metric-driven performance measures (TEF). The focus on environments in University 3.0 models allows support for learning and knowledge production processes to be considered, directly feeding into the design and curation of knowledge interfaces. In these kinds of learning environments, learners are supported by drawing from knowledges that are ever-present and all around us.

With a focus on interfaces between university and external sectors, these environments are more permeable to allow universities to be a key element in benefiting our knowledge economies. Partnerships are key for this trajectory, and in 2016 (Boehm, 2016a), I wrote that it might be useful to consider formalised partnership models that allow the barriers of these different spheres to be negotiated more effectively, to allow our institutions to become ever more permeable. This is, of course, where quadruple helix partnerships come in, as described in below chapters.

For all these aspects, the design of environments as permeable partnership ecosystems is necessary, and future-oriented study practices are already demonstrably adapting to this new learning environment. The importance – and challenges – of partnership-rich learning ecosystems feeding into forward-looking sustainable learning environments foregrounds the need and current trajectories within HE to move away from 'content' to 'environment'.

This focus on the learning environment builds upon a long history of learning concepts that educators and pedagogues have developed, as can be seen from Table 9.

These pedagogical tools demonstrate that we have already moved our own academic practices from a culture of specifying learning objectives, devising constructive alignments, specifying terminologies according to Bloom (Bloom, 1956), quality-assuring every single knowledge 'package' within a curriculum and validating its specific mode of assessment, to a more open consideration of learning environments and their related study practices, and how these need to be designed in order for learners to tap into their own

Table 9. Common Concepts Displaying Characteristics of a University 3.0.

Well-known educational concepts

Problem-based learning
Work-based learning
Collaborative learning
Peer learning
Personalised learning
Socially constructed learning
Authentic/Work-based learning
Inquiry/Research-based learning

Increasingly commonly-used concepts

Grand Challenge-led learning
(Simulated +) Real-life learning
Experiential learning

Still considered new....

Flipped classroom
Just-in-time learning
Phenomenon-based learning
Live briefs

passion of learning and drawing from the knowledges that surround them, both within the academic institutional boundaries and from outside. These environments will need to be designed to be permeable, and have both the academic dimensions with their deep knowledge domains and the applicability and cross-fertilisation opportunities of the world outside (See Boehm, 2019a).

In the innovation context, this matches concepts coined under the term Open Innovation 2.0 (Curley and Salmelin, 2015), but as facilitators of learning, we will need to consider what this paradigm shift means for our learning frameworks.

In our HE and FE institutions, many of us creative practitioners have already become in-betweeners, interconnectors, third culture practitioners and University 3.0 academics. We now live, breathe and work between music, art and technology, between practice and theory, between research, enterprise and innovation and we connect more than ever before with our surrounding communities.

As the subject disciplines around music, art, performance and media expanded, creative scholars transformed themselves from being owners of knowledge to curators of knowledge situated within an expanding and increasingly fragmented set of multi- and interdisciplinary knowledge fields. And once our knowledge society really took off, with its open platforms, its digital connectivity and its mass distribution without mediators, focus on providing quality HE provision was and still will need to increasingly be on learning environments (University 3.0), rather than specific knowledges (University 1.0), or the curation of fragmented areas of knowledge (University 2.0). It will all be about focussing on curating the environments where learning happens, and where knowledge is brought in from all around us (University 3.0).

Tableau #3 – 1997 to 2010: Cool Britannia and the Creative Industries

1997 was the year I arrived in Britain, or rather the United Kingdom; Glasgow, Scotland, to be exact. And the giddiness that swept the country when Labour came into power after a decade of austerity cannot be overstated. Getting to know my new country, it was clear that many around me really felt they deserved better, as the title of the Labour Manifesto in 1997 suggested (New Labour: Because Britain Deserves Better). And this giddiness had its core centre in British creative outputs, both in terms of the biggest creative industries of music and film, as well as the art scene of designers.

There is a picture collage I use in my lectures to give an impression of that time and its cultural giddiness. The images function for me as text, being able to read the societal shift happening at the time using the images and what they tell us, what they foreground or what they leave out. It provides a reading of how the perception of culture and the creative industry changed, and the concept of Cool Britannia is at the heart of it. The term and emerging style of 'Cool Britannia' seemed to capture the cultural renaissance of London at the time. In the collage, there are the usual images of Tony Blair celebrating his 1997 sweep to power, British flags flying and everyone cheering and waving. But also pictures of him with Noel Gallagher, having welcomed him to No 10 shortly after the election.[1] This was so obviously an intentional strategy as part of an effort to turn the United Kingdom even more into a cultural powerhouse or ride on the momentum that this cultural renaissance moment provided. Tony Blair understood the creative industries in their potential for soft power internationally, as well as nationally within the electorate. The collage also includes two magazine covers, one from *Newsweek* in 1996, situating London as the coolest city with its headlines of 'London Rules' and designer fashion that integrates an exorbitant Union Jack hat, and one from *Vanity Fair*, depicting Liam Gallagher and Patsy Kensit on a bedspread with and yes, again featuring an unmissable Union Jack motive.[2] The collage also includes images of Ginger

---

[1] Photograph: Rebecca Naden/PA https://www.theguardian.com/inequality/commentisfree/2017/jul/05/cool-britannia-inequality-tony-blair-arts-industry.
[2] 1997 Vanity Fair cover, depicting Liam Gallagher and Patsy Kensit. Photograph by Lorenzo Agius https://www.vanityfair.com/magazine/1997/03/london199703 (Last accessed 1 April 2022).

Spice Geri Halliwell wearing the iconic Union Jack dress at the 1997 Brit Awards, and images of movie posters announcing Mike Myer's *Austin Powers*, a sort of new quirky, fun James Bond in front of a backdrop of .... yes, again, Union Jack motives, and those from Danny Boyle's *Trainspotting*, which had been released featuring Britpop soundtrack.

Tableau #3. Cool Britannia (1997–2010).

Tableau and CPE	Cool Britannia and the Creative Industries (1997–2010)
Structural Selectivity	• Labour Creative Industry Policy 1997 onwards • Tony Blair, Prime Minister • Chris Smith, Secretary of State for Culture Media and Sport, DCMS
Discursive	• Emergence of the term and concepts of 'Cool Britannia' in public discourses (1997–1998) (Magazine Covers, Media, Film) • Labour Manifesto 1997: New Labour: Because Britain Deserves Better • Chris Smith, Creative Britain 1998 • DCMS, Creative Industries Mapping Document 1998 and 2001
Agency	• Tony Blair • Chris Smith • DCMS
Technological	• Influence of the digital in the creative industry strategy, with its inherent 'copyright-ability'.

Admittedly, Cool Britannia was a wave that had started before New Labour swept into power, building on the Swinging London of the 1960s, which also under Labour rose to international recognition for its sense of forward-looking fashion and individuality. But in the 1990s, two major industries rose to define British culture. First, the music industry was able to build on the successes of British greats, such as The Beatles, The Rolling Stones, Deep Purple, David Bowie and the Sex Pistols. Due to having access to the largest English-speaking markets worldwide, this sector continually grew to disproportional fame, compared to other countries with similar-size populations but located outside of the lucrative Anglo-American markets. A bit later, the UK film industry emerged, and it is notable that the biggest earliest film successes that fed into the Cool Britannia cinematic vibe often contained soundtracks from highly successful acts of the music sectors. *Four Weddings and a Funeral* (1994) is seen as an early portent of the new wave of British cinema and featured UK Single Chart hits, as did *Trainspotting*, released in 1996, featuring a soundtrack with pop hits from the 1970s to the Britpop era of Blur and Pulp.

These examples are significant, as they not only allow me personally to understand the drive I had to move from Germany to Britain, but it also denotes this subtle shift from a dominant type of cultural engagement of a Culture 1.0 kind, one based on patronage and (often unconscious) exclusionary practices, to a dominant type of cultural engagement more aligned to Culture 2.0 based on intellectual property and economic productivity and with it the support and rise of the creative industries.

The new government had finally caught on to the fact that money was to be made by being creative and was starting to provide funding for making 'Britain the leader in the new creative economy' (see Boehm, 2009).

Or, as Flew wrote in his book about the origins of the creative industries:

> *Labour came to power in Britain after 18 years of Conservative governments, headed by Margaret Thatcher and John Major, that had relentlessly pushed the privatisation of state-run enterprises, user-pays principles for access to government services, a self-reliant enterprise culture, and a general devaluation of the role of the public sector in*

*British economic and social life. This had been a
particularly cold climate for the arts, with peak
funding bodies such as the Arts Council of Great
Britain feeling underfunded and beleaguered.*

(Flew, 2012, p. 14)

Tension had already emerged between the for-profit and
the not-for-profit sectors, and artists themselves had become
targets for disdain in the mainstream media, with works that
had a critical, counter-cultural or avant-garde element being
routinely criticised as being wasteful of the public money they
may have received. Myerscough, in his 1988 book about *The
Economic Importance of the Arts in Britain*, suggested that
even by the time he wrote his book, it had become common to
argue the case for public support for the arts rather in terms
of their economic contribution (Myerscough, 1988).

*While the shift in power from the Conservatives
to Labour in 1997 was strongly welcomed in the
arts and cultural sectors, it had by this time
become common to argue for the value of the
arts and culture in Britain in economic terms,
and creative industries marked in one respect a
more innovative and influential way of doing
that.*

(Flew, 2012, p. 14)

I would suggest one of Labour's greatest achievements is
that when they finally got in, they speedily introduced substantial restructuring of how to fund the creative sectors and
the creative economy, confidently putting creativity at the
heart of their whole economic policy, that arts could no
longer be seen as a dispensable extra on the political agenda,
as Chris Smith, the new Secretary of State for Culture Media
and Sport in Blair's government suggested in a 1998 book
that outlined his policy (Smith, 1998) and that had industry
darling Damien Hirst print design on the jacket.

In this new world view, the creative sectors had suddenly moved from the fringes to the heart of the UK economy; they were reconceptualised as a key economic driver, providing the jobs of the future and maintaining our position in the world. This was already inherent in the Labour Party's Create the Future Manifesto, that the cultural industries 'are vital to the creation of jobs and the growth of our economy. The creative and media industries world-wide are growing rapidly – we must grasp the opportunities presented' (Labour Party, 1997).

The media sector here in the manifesto is still set apart from the Creative Industry as a whole and would be incorporated into the Creative Industry policies as being part of it, as it so heavily relied on IP and copyright alongside the other creative sectors, such as pop music, design and the film industry.

Chris Smith picked this up, suggesting that

> *Given the levels of growth already experienced in these fields, given the flow of changing technology and digitalisation, given our continuing ability to develop talented people, these creative areas are surely where many of the jobs and much of the wealth of the next century are going to come from.*
>
> *(Smith, 1998, p. 25)*

And of course by 2021, we had reached a stage where every eighth business is a creative business, proving him right. But Smith also changed the conceptualisation to sell his vision and ideology. As Garnham points out in his article about the emergence of the creative industries and its relationship to the media, and referring to the Creative Industries Mapping Document, first published in 1998 and republished in 2001, it defined who was in and was left out of the creative industries:

> *In the Mapping Document, the term 'creative' was chosen so that the whole of the computer software sector could be included. Only on this*

basis was it possible to make the claims about size and growth stand up. However, this inclusion had two valuable policy consequences for the interests involved. It enabled software producers and the major publishing and media conglomerates to construct an alliance with cultural workers, and with small-scale cultural entrepreneurs, around a strengthening of copyright protection.

(Garnham, 2005, p. 26)

The choice of 'creative', 'creativity' and 'Creative Industries' rather than 'cultural' was intentional and linked to aspects of intellectual property and the information society, and thus inclusive of media, games, video and journalism. This, as Garnham points out, influenced the set of economic analyses and policy arguments that were foregrounded from that point onwards, also in terms of economic returns (Garnham, 2005, p. 20).

This is quintessential Culture 2.0, with a focus on IP and copyright, digital mass reproducibility and economic productivity with substantial value being made. This then is not an uncontroversial moment in time, and one should remember that arts and creative industry-oriented economic policy can ideologically be so closely associated with basic key principles of a more general economic policy; any tensions between the two also point toward the ideologies underpinning basic political policy stances in relation to the balance between the economy and society. Many key organisations, in hindsight, have criticised this strategy. NESTA stated in their 2016 Provocation Document about the lack of a Cultural Policy and highlighted the problems with the New Labour definition of the Creative Industries:

We suggest that the conflation of culture with creative industries since 1997 has harmed both cultural policy and creative industries policy in the UK. We propose that an official definition of

*the cultural sector and the production of govern-
ment statistics to support such a definition will
help to clarify creative industries policy and create
a much needed opportunity to revisit the scope
and nature of cultural policy.*

(NESTA, 2016)

NESTA, by that time, was able to see that the definition used did not explicitly use or measure the value of the cultural sector, and were with that disappearing from policy attention, and thus sought to add to the creative industries a separate new concept around a 'creative economy' rather than a pre-scribed list of 'creative industries', as 'stakes for the UK are much higher than the fate of individual industries' (NESTA, 2016, p. 4. See also Newbigin in eds. S. Cunningham & T. Flew, 2019, pp. 21–22).

But this perspective suggests a rather conservative view of 'the arts' remaining in a set Culture 1.0 world and the commercial sector, the creative industries, remaining in Culture 2.0. Ignoring the substantial interaction between these types of cultural engagement and the creative professionals that easily move in and out of these two types of cultural engagements, I have found this rather a conservative, regressive perspective on how to best allow both the creative economy and creative industries to have the most collective impact on both society health and economic wealth.

But this view does have its supporters. The tensions arose early on, between the 'industry' and the 'artistic sector', and they are apparent when McGuigan writes that 'as the cultural industries grew in the mid-twentieth century, national cultural policies came to be formulated primarily as a defence of art against the commercialisation, industrialisation and commodification of culture' (Mcguigan, 2004, p. 175).

Using lenses of Culture 1.0, 2.0 and 3.0, I would suggest there is a benefit in a diversity of these different cultural forms, and with the diversity of cultural engagements also comes resilience. Having funding or policy predominantly focussed on Culture 1.0 results in elitism and exclusivity, as we have seen so often in the art world, which still struggles with the fact that it is so white and so upper middle class. Having funding or policy predominately focused on Culture 2.0 creates a highly neo-liberal, worker-exploitative model, as we have seen in the record industries in Britain, where creative producers, composers and songwriters struggle to get by whilst large commercial organisations, such as labels, exploit their standing and power. This is a simplification of what is going on in relation to the #brokenrecord campaigns, but looking on the big scale, it vaguely holds up.

I do not know what a world would look like that might focus solely on Culture 3.0 type engagements, but I do know it would be more accessible and less exclusionary. However, I would want to see our creative societies move towards a balance between these types of cultural phenomena and governments to consider this when formulating investment strategies. Culture 1.0, with its patronage, and therefore artists allowed to go deep into their self-reflective practice, often results in highly innovative, experimental and novel creative practices, more so than Culture 2.0, which often has a tendency to cater to a market, and more so than Culture 3.0 where often there is not one individual artist, but rather a collectively owned process. A balance and diversity of these different phenomena of cultural engagement should be at the heart of any creative economy and cultural policy that aims to have both social and economic resilience as its aim.

But back in 1997, and once Labour was in power, it was now under the highly successful vision of New Labour, an ideology formulating centre-left market economics and its 'third way' between capitalism and socialism, influenced by Anthony Giddens' 'Third Way' (1998). Several policy introductions happened quite quickly.

The Department of National Heritage (DNH) became the Department for Culture, Media and Sport (DCMS). Policy focus moved away from high art and high culture towards an economically driven policy for the creative industries, and one could argue that this represents a shift of a department steeped in Culture 1.0 to one prioritising Culture 2.0 (see also Boehm, 2019c).

Additionally, the Creative Industries Task Force (CITF) was set up under the leadership of Chris Smith, setting out to map the current activity in those sectors deemed to be a part of the UK creative industries, measuring their contribution to Britain's overall economic performance through its Creative Industries Mapping Document (DCMS, 2001) and identifying policy measures that would promote their further development. As Chris Smith, in an *Independent* article at the time, commented:

> *When the then-named Department of National Heritage was set up in 1992, the tabloids called it the Ministry of Fun and the Ministry of Free Tickets. I wanted the department to be serious as well as fun. I decided to set up a task force on the economic potential of the creative industries.*
> (Smith, in: Koenig, 1998)

The Government's vision at that time was of 'a Britain in 10 years' time, where the local economies in our biggest cities are driven by creativity' (DCMS, 2008). But in the naughts, creativity – and with it the creative sector – was seen to be important. The government's 1998 Creative Industries Mapping Document mapped all industries that can be associated with the 'creative professional', and it made it clear that the vision is one where our industrialised economies of the future will only succeed if we manage to bring in processes that support creativity and the creative professional. And with it, 'the creative industries moved from the fringes to the mainstream' (DCMS, 2001). Measuring its already existent economic performance was important for making a persuasive case, and therefore the IP focused scope of the concept of the Creative Industries, which allowed it to include the media industries and publishing. The Mapping Document identified the creative industries as constituting a large and growing component of the UK economy, employing 1.4 million people and generating an estimated £60 billion a year in economic value added, or about 5% of total UK national income at that time. The updated 2001 document takes account of regional attributes, such as clustering.

5

ARTS IN UNIVERSITY LIFE: A SHORT PHENOMENOLOGY

Universities carefully position various interfaces between different levels of learners, different types of communities and different disciplines. This careful positioning is a process of curating interfaces, with the facilitation of learning being at the heart of this process rather than the acquisition or transfer of knowledge itself. This nuanced distinction is one that Thomas and Brown (2011) have written about in their 'New Culture of Learning', which (oversimplified here) suggests we, in the universities, need to focus more on developing and specifying environments in which learning happens or is afforded, rather than focusing on knowledge content with specific learning objectives. This is also a prerequisite for our future Universities 3.0.

As an academic within the arts who is passionate about the concept of the public university and who perceives these institutions as regional hubs and anchors, the need for creative interfaces between academia and society also raises questions about how we support our current and future talent to be impactful in society with creative means. How do we in academia 'get connected', and how do we facilitate this in the curriculum.

University art schools are some of the biggest patrons of creative thinking and practice, recognised even by the Arts Council when suggesting that

> *Higher education institutions are playing an increas-*
> *ingly vital role as custodians and champions of arts*
> *and culture in towns and cities across the country.*
> *They support the development of young talent. They*
> *lead on research of national and international signifi-*
> *cance. And their investment in arts and culture helps to*
> *build a sense of place. Universities, colleges and con-*
> *servatoires have come to be powerful investors in their*
> *local areas, in the knowledge that a strong cultural offer*
> *makes our towns and cities great places to live, work*
> *and study.*
>
> (Henley, 2016)

Our learning environments will need to become more permeable between universities and external sectors to allow universities to remain a key element in benefiting our knowledge economies in the future. It is useful to consider formalised partnership models that allow the barriers of these different spheres to be negotiated more effectively to afford the 'ivory tower' to become more permeable; For example Etzkowitz's model of university-industry-government partnership, the triple helix (Etzkowitz, 2008) and the expanded quadruple helix (Carayannis and Campbell, 2012a) to include civil society organisations and with it universities' own civic engagements.

Already back in 2009, Watson (Watson, 2009, 2014, 2011) had started to foreground this latter role; his concept of the 'engaged university' proposes that social enterprise and the not-for-profit sector should be considered within the helix model. These quadruple partnerships are evidenced to better support innovation, but they also allow innovation to happen in a non-linear, collaborative manner with overlapping processes of basic research, application and development, creating what has been called a 'socially distributed knowledge' (Gibbons, 1994) or a (Mode 3) 'Innovation Ecosystem' (Carayannis and Campbell, 2012).

Within the undergraduate learning frameworks, these ideas have been comprehensively explored and conceptualised within an undergraduate and postgraduate context in Fung's Connected Curriculum (Fung, 2017), which established a framework that inherently and explicitly connects research with our learning environments.

Seeing it through my two lenses, this connects University 3.0 with Culture 3.0.

One could suggest that the arts in the academy have always had it easier to be more permeable, to be more connected and to focus on the interfaces between various communities. Art always asks for audiences, and additionally, Culture 3.0 affords participation. Thus the arts have already established many encultured practices that could be seen to fall into innovation ecosystems and connected curricula (Boehm, 2016a), with its practice-oriented methodologies that often have a built-in impact right from the start. However, this also has made it harder to evidence this connectivity or its impact. Long-established practices were taken for granted: evidencing impact explicitly is hard for creatives. We all know it works, but we cannot seem to easily say how, why and by how much and for whom.

Having said this, there is a long tradition and high critical awareness of co-production, authorship, co-ownership and immersive arts. All these elements are traits in Sacco's Culture 3.0 (2011), but, furthermore, it points towards an understanding of art as not a distinct but rather an immersive ever-presence of art all around us.

I would even suggest that, to such an extent, the concept of the creative industries becomes problematic as a distinct sector. Various governments have had to expand the definitions of the Creative Industries, as creativity has become a key skill for many sectors beyond the traditional creative industries. As an example, the latest DCMS definitions contained in the 2018 Creative Industries Sector Deal (BEIS, 2018) differentiate but include in various figures not only 'Creative Occupations within the creative industries' but also 'Non-creative/support jobs within the creative industries' and 'Creative occupations outside the creative industries'. In a service-focused economy, and one that believes in big-is-better, it is a consequence that it will largely focus on IP and copyright, and creativity lies at the heart of ensuring the viability of wealth through IP.

Similar movements have happened with other sectors; the IT sector has become almost indistinguishable from other industries, as IT has become pervasive and innovation draws more often from the novelty of how communities are connected (through technologies) but less on the novelty of the technologies being developed. And this connectivity, often through art and technology, paves the way for Culture 3.0 with its heightened potential for large-scale cultural participation.

1. UNIVERSITY ART-SCHOOLS AS DRIVERS FOR CULTURAL AND ECONOMIC GROWTH

Cultural participation has a demonstrable but indirect effect on Innovation, Welfare, Social Cohesions, Entrepreneurship, Local Identity and the Knowledge Economy. And as we will see below, University Art schools demonstrably contribute directly or indirectly to almost half of a region's cultural engagement points. But when art norms and value systems for the arts are still prioritising a Culture 1.0 patronage model, with small audiences, value absorption and its own gatekeepers, the engagement types provide a barrier to achieving these indirect effects on society.

To remind ourselves, Sacco suggested that Europe is still hung up on Culture 1.0, and this is suggested to stifle our innovative potential by reducing access. There is substantial evidence of this effect. As the EU Cultural and Creative Cities Monitor report published in 2009 suggests:

> 'In the literature, two main mechanisms can be identified through which culture would contribute to this new economy.
>
> 1. First, the 'Cultural and Creative Sectors (CCS) mechanism', demonstrated by the increasing weight of the CCS in national GDPs and international trade (KEA, 2006; D. Throsby, 2001, 2008; UNCTAD, 2010, 2013).
>
> 2. Second, the 'cultural amenities mechanism', confirmed by the capacity of culture-related amenities such as arts centres and cultural heritage sites, but also aesthetics and lifestyles, to attract population, especially the high-skilled (Carlino and Saiz, 2008; Falck et al.,

2011; Nelson et al., 2016) as well as leisure visitors
(Richards, 1996; Romão et al., 2018) to cities.
                              (Merola et al., 2019b, p. 90).

The Cultural and Creative Cities Monitor was introduced in
2017 and, in its biannual installations, is a 'new tool to monitor and
assess the performance of 'Cultural and Creative Cities' in Europe
vis-à-vis their peers using both quantitative and qualitative data"
(p. 19). With the data of more than 150 European Creative cities
(and growing), this first of bi-annual reports was able to prove that
'culture is ultimately associated with European cities' economic
wealth' and that 'culture and economic wealth mutually reinforce
each other' (Merola et al., 2019b, p. 89). Art and Culture have a
large part to play here, especially because:

> *Culture is not simply a large and important sector of the*
> *economy, it is a 'social software' that is badly needed to*
> *manage the complexity of contemporary societies and*
> *economies in all of its manifold implications.*
>
>   *(Sacco, 2014)*

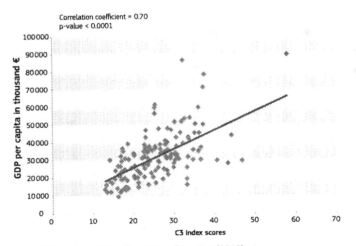

Fig. 4. Cultural and Creative Cities Monitor (2019).

As a Figure (Fig. 4) from the 2019 installation of the monitor
suggests and using 29 indicators within three dimensions to

calculate a so-called C3 index, wealth is linked to creative and cultural engagement.

As a note, the C3 index here is an index made up of three sub-indices, nine dimensions and 29 indicators, developed in consultation with policymakers, academics and practitioners in the field of culture and creativity (see Table 10). Of these, three are directly linked to universities, and a further 12 are closely linked, making a conservative estimate of a whopping 51% directly or closely linked to a university presence, below indicated in italics.

The monitor covers three major facets of a 'Cultural and Creative City':

- 'Cultural Vibrancy', which measures the cultural 'pulse' of a city in terms of cultural infrastructure and participation in culture;

- 'Creative Economy', which captures how the cultural and creative sectors contribute to a city's economy in terms of employment, job creation and innovation; and

- 'Enabling Environment', which identifies the tangible and intangible assets that help cities attract creative talent and stimulate cultural engagement. The methodology is laid out in ANNEX A: The Cultural and Creative Cities Monitor methodology in 10 steps (Merola et al., 2019a).

The GDP here is used as a proxy for economic wealth; the authors note the challenges around this model and provide additional calculations to provide confidence in the model. Discussions in recent times have also put the whole validity of GDP as a measure of economic growth in question, as with its aggregate essence, it does not account for wealth distribution, quality of life, or environmental aspects, so it ignores stratification in society in terms of wealth, health or productivity. However, in the absence of a better-accepted model, and considering that one can assume that when using better measures for economic wealth that take account of wealth distribution, the correlation to C3 index scores should only increase when taking unequal distribution into account, specifically considering that the C3 indices do take cultural engagement (e.g. cultural distribution and distance to cultural facilities) into account.

Table 10. 29 Indicators of the Cultural and Creative Cities Monitor.[a]

Cultural Vibrancy	Creative Economy	Enabling Environment
D1.1 Cultural Venues and Facilities	D2.1 Creative and Knowledge-based Jobs	D3.1 Human Capital and Education
• sights and landmarks	• Jobs in arts, culture and entertainment	• Graduates in arts and humanities
• Museums and art galleries	• Jobs in media and communication	• Graduates in ICT
• Cinemas	• Jobs in other creative sectors	• Average appearances in university rankings
• Concert and music halls		
• Theatres		
D1.2 Cultural Participation and Attractiveness	D2.2 Intellectual Property and Innovation	D3.2 Openness, Tolerance and Trust
• Tourist overnight stays	• ICT patent applications	• Foreign graduates
• Museum visitors	• Community design applications	• Foreign-born population
• cinema attendance		• Tolerance of foreigners
• satisfaction with cultural facilities		• Integration of foreigners
		• People trust

Table 10. (Continued)

Cultural Vibrancy	Creative Economy	Enabling Environment
	D2.3 New Jobs in Creative Sectors	D3.3 Local and International Connections
	• *Jobs in new arts, culture and entertainment enterprises* • *Jobs in new media and communication enterprises* • *Jobs in new enterprises in other creative sectors*	• Accessibility to passenger flights • Accessibility by road • Accessibility by rail
		D3.4 Quality of Governance
		• Quality of the local governance

[a]Italics denote indices directly or indirectly linked to universities.
Source: Merola et al. (2019).

More interesting and relevant to the issue of regional impact are the findings in relation to the following:

- Correlation remains valid regardless of the size of the cities
- Correlation remains valid regardless of the fact if the city is a capital city or not; it is not a significant determinant
- However, cities with better weather conditions, an abundance of parks, a lower presence of manufacturing and more historic landmarks are perceived as more attractive (2019b, p. 90)

And this has specific significance for medium-sized and small post-industrial second-order cities, such as Stoke-on-Trent, Turku, Aarhus, Tampere and similar cities, as their regeneration and industrial strategy thus should ideally incorporate a strong cultural strategy in order to maximise the mutual benefits of economic productivity and social well-being. Stoke-on-Trent, for instance, as the quintessential creative city, but similar to many other 'left-behind' post-industrial UK cities, can make use of its creative and cultural heritage, its historic buildings assets, and its green spaces as well as plenty of knowledge-driven institutions.

And this is where universities can play a large role, as with their extensive partnership work, they really have the ability to tie together local government, civil society, creative actors and creative industry to their own innovation and learning focused academic communities. Universities have one of the largest human capital in the form of staff, students and researchers. But specifically, students, when part of learning environments that cross institutional boundaries between inside and outside the institution, with experiential learning embedding links to the professional world, provide a large opportunity for learning on all sides.

So maximising the opportunity for learning environments to incorporate quadruple helix model partnerships and open innovation ecosystems, allowing students to learn the richness of moving into Culture 3.0 to maximise their societal impact, and being facilitated for doing all this by a conceptual shift of university education of what I have conceptualised as University 3.0, allows learning to be maximised whilst economic productivity and society well-being is increased as well.

One of the two case studies I developed for a Leverhulme Fellowship (Boehm, 2021 (not yet published)) comes from Turku in Finland, evidenced as having high creative participation of their citizens and significant cultural engagement (Boehm, 2021). When considering how a university-housed arts provision has become so impactful to its associated communities, as I suggested in my work that both the Arts Academy at TUAS University as well as the research-intensive Turku University have been demonstrably beneficial to the health and well-being and the cultural vibrancy of a place as well as influencing national take-up of arts and culture as part of a national strategic policy for society, then the 2011 European Capital of Culture is repeatedly mentioned. And this was the case in my interviews, as many of the trajectories that can be seen within various research and innovation projects can be traced back to a direction-setting that started with the city's application to become the European Capital of Culture.

As one of the academic and cultural leads of the bid, Andersson writes:

> *Even though most European Capitals of Culture (ECoC) have been university cities, academic research has seldom played much of a role in their programmes. The case of the Finnish city of Turku, European Capital of Culture 2011, is different.*
>
> *(Andersson and Ruoppila, 2011)*

Significantly, the universities and the city took the opportunity to design a large number of partnership projects that included city actors, citizens and universities, all involved in co-creating research output, educational content and cultural processes. PhD and Masters students were targeted to support this process, and the evaluation of the programme itself, running from 2010 to 2016, was led by the University of Turku under Professor Harri Andersson (Andersson and Ruoppila, 2011).

The result can be seen demonstrably in the latest EU Cultural and Creative Cities Monitor. In the 2019 cities monitor (Merola et al., 2019b), Turku, a medium-sized post-industrial second-order city, ended up being (in its population category M-medium):

- 1st/57 (1st out of 57) in Europe in terms of Quality of Creative and Cultural Governance

- 6th/57 in Europe in terms of Intellectual Property and Innovation

- 7th/57 in Europe in terms of Human Capital and Education

- 9th/57 in Europe in terms of cultural participation and attractiveness

- 20th/57 in Europe in terms of Openness, Tolerance and Trust

And thus, having great scores in the three dimensions of the framework (related to cities of the same population).

- Enabling environment = 8th out of 57 in Europe

- Cultural vibrancy = 11th out of 57 in Europe

- Creative economy = 24th out of 57 in Europe

A second case study came from Aarhus in Denmark, also a second-order city in the large category, which in its population category (L) is:

- 1st/57 in Europe in terms of Quality of Creative and Cultural Governance

- 6th/57 in Europe in terms of Intellectual Property and Innovation

- 5th/57 in Europe in terms of Openness, Tolerance and Trust

- 8th/57 in Europe in terms of cultural participation and attractiveness

- 29th/57 in Europe in terms of Human Capital and Education

And thus, having great scores in the three dimensions of the framework (related to cities of the same population).

- Cultural vibrancy = 9th out of 57 in Europe

- Creative economy = 24th out of 57 in Europe
- Enabling environment = 11th out of 57 in Europe

Both cities have been European Capitals of Culture. Both cities have various higher education (HE) institutions, so it is worthwhile to consider the learning environments that universities develop, and that demonstrably have a positive impact on their localities and regions. For me, the question from these case studies was to look into what makes especially those academic and learning environments so impactful. Is there something we can learn when we design our educational environments for our learning communities or the way we bring in our partnerships to benefit both learning and knowledge production? Universities, as anchors in their region, often hold the biggest human capital in medium to small-sized cities and become real powerhouses of innovation, productivity and creativity. Our students and learners are the biggest part of this community.

2. ART EDUCATION IN HIGHER EDUCATION

There is already a substantial shift of thinking noticeably about how we facilitate learning, and not just in our university-housed art schools. The discourse has shifted from the understanding that governments have moved the HE sector to adopt specific impact agendas that took specifically regional prosperity into account to collaborative and cooperative learning, to experiential learning frameworks embedded at an institutional level, to challenge-led learning and flipped classrooms, often without using this term. So it is exactly those structural, systemic, procedural or pedagogical characteristic more akin to the University 3.0 model that makes these kinds of processes in universities more impactful. However, understanding the current university sector that still sees itself more akin to University 1.0 or even 2.0 models, it becomes clear that there are tensions based on some basic premises attached to these conceptualisations, that knowledge is the key asset that lecturers and universities hold or own. These tensions are the least dominant in the creative disciplines that have a long evolution towards focusing on processes.

This also signifies a move towards a new way of conceptualising learning environments, one that moves from a culture of specifying learning objectives, devising constructive alignments, specifying in terminologies of Bloom, quality-assuring every single knowledge within a curriculum and validating its specific mode of assessment to a more open consideration of learning environments, and how these need to be designed in order for learners to tap into their own passion of learning and drawing themselves from the knowledges that are all around them, both within this academic environment and from outside. These environments are increasingly designed to be permeable themselves, and they hold both the academic dimensions with their deep knowledge domains and the applicability and cross-fertilisation opportunities of the world outside.

In the learning context, this matches concepts coined under the term University 3.0 (and in the innovation context under the term Open Innovation 2.0). The move from formalised and structured learning objects (Uni 2.0) to formalised structured learning environments (Uni 3.0) has only just begun, but there are examples where this has always happened in practice, specifically in the art provisions within those universities that truly want to be connected to their communities.

Art provisions in the university spaces can help with this connectivity. Art is inherently permeable, constantly asking for an audience. Its actors live and survive through being social and business entrepreneurs within a seamless continuum. University-housed Art-schools allow institutions to make use of art's inherently permeable nature to create intentional and curated interfaces between what is within a university and what is outside of its boundaries. Art, more often than not, lives in the intersections between university, society, industry and government.

Both art and culture are intractably linked to humanity and society, and so it is also when considering where art 'happens' within the academic sectors. It is too simple to think of art in HE as simply one subject discipline, as it is often much more than this.

As a start, a simple list might demonstrate the intractably diffused nature of where art 'lives' in our universities:

- Undergraduate and post-graduate taught degrees situated within the creative disciplines,

- post-graduate research degrees and PhDs,

- artistic practices as research and research into arts,

- student-experience focused extra-curricular arts offer,

- creative student and staff enterprise,

- university-housed public arts centres,

- arts used for widening participation related activities,

- creatively oriented schools outreach programmes,

- community engagement,

- creatively curated exhibitions of non-arts research etc

In a former University, where I had the privilege to not only be the Head of a Department for almost a decade but also chair the committee of a publicly co-funded Arts Centre housed within the department, we could list various dimensions that catered for various communities, each with its vested interests and agendas. This was summarised as (Boehm et al., 2014b) (Table 11):

Table 11. University-Housed Arts Centre Agendas.[a]

Agendas/Vested Interests/Drivers		Funding sources
Arts Education Student Experience Employability	Inward facing	Largely department funded
Research / Impact Agendas Enterprise / Income Generation WP / Community-University / University as Anchors	to	Largely University funded
Generating New Work / Supporting New Talent Public Cultural Asset / Cultural Policy Arts Sector Development	Outward facing	Substantially externally funded (ACE and Ticket sales)

[a]Carver in Boehm et al. (2014b).

Any arts department will have a different equilibrium between inward and outward-facing agendas, and this depends on various internal and external factors. In a very short study undertaken in 2013 (in Boehm et al., 2014b), Carver interviewed the artistic directors of four academically housed, small-scale live arts centres in the United Kingdom's northwest, which demonstrated how diverse the different foci of these centres are, from one centre (Centre A) being seen foremost as a resource for and benefitting students to another (Centre B) with a more dominant outward-looking community impact and research impact agenda. Carver categorised these different 'flavours' of arts departments as (1) Quasi-autonomous cultural assets; (2) HEI experience enhancers; (3) Departmental Resource; and (4) Curated Contemporary Practice (Carver, 2014) (Fig. 5).

The decision of these kinds of positioning has consequences of choices of where to position staff; arts or music directors of universities that see their music offer primarily serving interests of the whole university or of the wider community will more likely

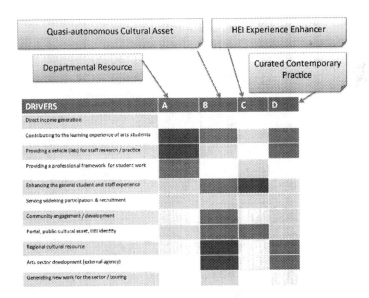

Fig. 5. Different Foci for Arts Departments (2014)[1].

position these linked but separate from the music or arts departments that focus on teaching. Whereas institutions that see arts activities also benefitting research agendas or student experience will more likely want to position key staff involved in the running and leading of arts activities within academic departments to ensure the link to research and student experience agendas can be made easily. There are pros and cons to each choice. This demonstrates that depending on external funding contexts and internal strategic considerations both at departmental and institutional level, departments consciously chose to situate themselves between, on the one hand, offering an only student-focused and experience-enhancing cultural offer, or on the other end a fully resourced public arts centre open to communities beyond university boundaries.

More often than not, art schools will have situated themselves somewhere in between these two extremes. And additional layers of staff interests (such as public performative output based on research or income generation) and community interests (arts venue collaboration with regional arts organisations) will feed into this, as well as another dimension of disciplinary provision a department may have, from creative writing, theatre, music, drama, dance or community arts. And last but not least, funding structures have their own influence in making some choices of positioning more available than others. Whether a department has a fully devolved budget, including staffing costs, or whether departments only have a much smaller operational budget, these things matter as well. If decision-making on substantial expenditure is not devolved down to those communities in which academics and learners are the beneficiaries of that investment, then it can be much harder to internally persuade other managers of the benefits, specifically when financial resources are already stretched.

Tableau #4: A University-Housed Arts Centre

To understand the day-to-day realities of managing these creative interfaces between arts and academia, I will draw from a case study that I published in 2014 (Boehm, 2016a, p. 40ff), looking at the no-longer-existing Department of Contemporary Arts at MMU Cheshire, closed in the process of Manchester Metropolitan University's efforts to consolidate its campuses to Manchester. To readers that have arts provision in their departments or universities, much will sound familiar, but looking at it with a Culture 3.0 lens and considering the phenomena of Arts in Academia will hopefully provide some new insights (Tableau #4).

Tableau # 4. A University-Housed Arts Centre (2016).

Tableau & CPE	University-Housed Arts Centre
Structural selectivity	• A university-housed arts centre with its five functions
Discursive	• Arts centre committee reports, • Departmental documentation, website and public panel debates, • REF 2014 (REF, 2014)
Agency	• Head of department • Artistic director • Arts centre director • Committees and communities contributing to decisions of the centre
Technological	• Dissemination and communication tools, e.g. Social media, promotional materials and website

The Cheshire faculty had had a long-standing arts provision, as well as a public arts offer that went back to the 'Cultural Policy' of the old Crewe and Alsager College of Higher Education in the early eighties. The Axis Arts Centre and the Department of Contemporary Arts in which it was housed had been long known for their commitment to contemporary arts practices and practice-as-research. From its webpage, it laid out:

> *Axis Arts Centre aims to promote the best emergent, national and international small-scale touring contemporary theatre, live art, contemporary*

dance, performance writing, new music and installation.[2]

Axis had programmed some of the world's leading artists, including Michael Nyman, Wayne McGregor, Les Ballets C de la B (Belgium), Frantic Assembly, Odin Teatret (Denmark), Goat Island (Chicago), Forced Entertainment, Théâtre de Complicite, Tim Crouch, Benjamin Zephaniah and Lemn Sissay.

Like many academic arts departments, the department itself had a diverse undergraduate and post-graduate portfolio of provisions: Music Technology, Popular Music, Composition, Performance, Intermedia, Live Arts, Drama, Theatre, Dance, Creative Writing and Community Arts. There was a strong relationship with the creative sector (both for-profit and not-for-profit), and it saw itself as a department continually influencing the creative sector in Britain and beyond, specifically through the vehicle of the Axis Arts Centre.

The academic and research-active community was relatively large; in 2016, it had 25 members of permanent staff, another 40 associate lecturers and instrumental/vocal tutors and another 40 post-graduate research students, seven performance and digital media technicians, and various student interns, ambassadors and regular student volunteers for arts centre activities. Since 2008 it had been based in a new, purpose-built facility in Crewe in Cheshire, including music studios, sound recording studios, post-production, project spaces, specialist media suites for both audio and video work, and theatre and dance spaces.

The department had the not-for-profit cultural enterprise, the Axis Arts Centre, in its midst, co-funded by the Arts Council and housed within the Department, which had been programming for more than 25 years and had a reputation for its work with acclaimed companies and practitioners in live contemporary arts practices and benefitting the sector in

[2]Axis Arts Centre at the Department of Contemporary Arts, MMU Cheshire. http://www.cheshire.mmu.ac.uk/dca/axis-arts-centre/14/11/2016/.

providing a rurally based venue for live contemporary arts in a region that was known to have a low engagement for contemporary live art.

The challenging role between a public arts centre and an offer that supports student learning can be seen in the following quote by its Director, Jodie Gibson, who was during its lifetime a full member of staff within the department, the ... *AAC is a public arts centre and a resource for audiences in the region, a key function of the centre is to offer supplementary learning, research and performance opportunities for students within the Department of Contemporary Arts (DCA), which AAC is housed within. According to the department's strategy, recruitment material and induction sessions for new students, engagement in arts centre activity is considered important for the experience of post-graduate and under-graduate students, specifically in relation to enhancing and expanding their knowledge, skills, professional contacts and practice in the sector* (Gibson, 2014).

One of the examples of academic departments balancing inward- and outward-facing interests is that the process of running a public Arts Centre was integral to the research activities, the curation of programmes and the running of the arts centre was a research theme with staff expertise in the department; from a staff PhD on curation with the apt title: 'The Monster in our Midst: The Materialisation of Practice-as-Research in the British Academy' (see Linden, 2012) to research on live arts curation and its relationship to new knowledge for art practices (Linden and Mackenzie, 2009), to organisational change in small-scale arts centres (Gibson, 2014), to the phenomenological research of arts in academia (Boehm, 2016) on which this book is actually based and represents a much-expanded version. Thus the exercise of choosing artists that are perceived to be contemporary was interrogated within a research enquiry, as were the questions of what makes arts practices unique or what unique processes artists apply to ensure their artwork and performances are innovative. The Arts Centre itself was a subject of study, but it also was a platform where creative production could be staged, specifically those that had come out of a research process, out of a line of enquiry for new knowledge around creative practices.

But beyond providing an arts offer and a platform for work derived from practice-as-research by staff and post-graduate research students, it was also student-focused. It provided a learning environment as well as employment opportunities by recruiting students to be front of house staff, commissioning students to perform work or allowing the Arts Centre to be an object of study for their own undergraduate research projects.

Thus for the department, and for most academically housed small-scale arts centres, there is the equilibrium of sustainability to be met in an ever-shifting climate and agendas, thus not a straightforward measurement considering that the activities are often funded through a variety of sources altogether, as laid out in Table 11. This makes it a balancing act between inward-facing agendas, such as student learning, student experience and student employment, and outward-facing interests, such as generating new work, being a public cultural asset and developing the sector. In-between those two extremes are staff facing agendas, such as allowing an Arts Centre to support research and impact agendas, generating income or utilising the centre as an interface to allow the university to become a cultural anchor in its region.

There is a vital difference between an academically housed arts centre and a public arts centre, just as there is a difference between an academic-arts-practitioner and an (non-academically engaging) artist. The obligation, remit or privilege of universities to make knowledge explicit, to allow knowledge to be transferred over time and space, sets arts academics apart from artists outside of academia. It is the basic but public knowledge remit that includes learning, teaching and research as one continuum.

Thus there is the affordance and obligation not to just create unique artwork but to allow society to have an insight into the processes that make this artwork unique. The new knowledge here might be inherent within the artwork, and the artwork can be seen as evidence of a process that applies innovative practice, but the new knowledge from an academic point of view resides, and can only be made explicit when considering the process rather than merely the artefact, as practice-as-research in the arts inherently does (see Nelson, 2013).

Thus there is a continuum of inward- to outward-facing vested interests, often logically (but not always) aligned to the resources of funding linked to activities and their associated agendas. It is this balance of inward to outward facing interests and associated communities which creates a sustainable equilibrium. How this equilibrium manifests itself depends on various factors.

To balance these factors within the Axis Arts Centre, there were five explicitly defined functions that clarified how much its ongoing activities are linked to existing remits as a learning community (see Table 12 below).

Table 12. An Example of an Arts Centre and Its Five Functions.[a]

Functions

Learning environment	'Law students buy books; performance art students need to experience live contemporary arts'
Employability and student success	'Platforming current and past student success, providing professional employment opportunities in the creative sector'
Student experience	'Getting more value for your money, placement and volunteering opportunities to understand the sector, work experience in a professional context within the department'
Research and knowledge exchange	'Impact agendas, public platforms for our staff research and professional practices, attracting research funding in the arts'
Community engagement and outreach	'Providing curated and intentional interfaces between the university and the public, collaborations for creative sector projects innovation and research-led'

[a]Unpublished report to the University, Gibson, 2012.

These functions can sometimes be more difficult to understand by university executives who might not have an in-depth understanding of the embedded and holistic nature of the role of arts within a creative learning community. It allows the fragmentation of professional HE sector functions, conceptualised under terms (and support sections) of employability, widening participation, student experience, learning support, research-informed learning, enterprise etc., to disappear into a more intricately interconnected and multi-directionally beneficial wider learning community with a creative practice and its related knowledges at its core.

More easily understood by HE managers, who more often come from the sciences than the arts, might be the analogy that academically housed small arts centres can be seen as similar to what labs are to engineering students, or what books are to business students. They allow students to experience the contemporary live form of a practice they are currently studying. Live art is here the text. They also provide opportunities for students to engage professionally as artists, front-of-house staff, project managers or volunteers, thus having an embedded employability agenda whilst also allowing student successes to be celebrated by platforming the best of their work.

For staff, similar embedded agendas can be supported through academically housed arts centres, practising artist-academics thus have a public platform, allowing research impact agendas to be addressed. Through curated knowledge events, insights into their practice (and praxis) can be related to a public that is increasingly interested in process.

Having a professional arts centre run by staff and students, as part of everyday learning, research and knowledge exchange activities, also allows a community of academics to continually practice what they teach, be practitioners informed by professional practice through the processes of running a publicly co-funded arts centre. It meets enterprise agendas by attracting funding that supports our students and staff through commissions, creative projects, or community-university partnership projects. Lastly, but not least important, simply by allowing this wider learning community to engage in contemporary practices, from undergraduate to professional and PhD level, it provides a cultural asset for the external communities. Together, it creates a curated and intentional interface (or sets of interfaces) between a university and a local/regional/national/global public.

The above can be seen as structural constraints revolving around balancing inwards and outwards facing activities, e.g. the main structural tool for this being the five seasons support the five functions of (1) Learning Environment; (2) Employability and Student Success; (3) Student Experience; (4) Research and Knowledge Exchange; and (5) Community Engagement and Outreach.

The University thus made use of a university-housed arts centre to make its core activity of education more effective, to make itself more permeable, to have more engagement with its surrounding community, to increase its research prestige and to have more impact on its region.

The increase in this use of arts in the academy suggests a shift from University 2.0 to University 3.0 models, or in other words, an increase in the importance of civic university agendas.

But this also points to some of the tensions and threats, particularly for arts in HE within the UK HE system. With the disappearance of the mainly publicly funded university, due to the shift from a taxpayer-funded sector to a private student-funded system, these multidirectional benefits are more difficult to capture when fragmentation of functions has become more the norm. A decision-maker only wanting to see an academically housed arts centre as an enterprise activity, being able to make its own profits, will not be able to exploit its benefits for the learning by students. Similarly, increasingly if we allow learners to only see the assessed work as the evidence of their learning, and if learners perceive mainly the classroom lecture as the service they are paying 9k fees for, learners will be in danger of seeing everything else as a university indulging in its own interests.

Thus the same strength of this holistic curated interface between academia and the public is also its weakness. Even when the multiplicity of benefits to students is understood, when the equilibrium of balancing different agendas is in danger of shifting, as it would do, for example with the expansion of activities, resources or audiences, a multitude of stakeholders are affected. And taking out one part of the whole, as for instance the professional performance programme from the centre, would leave a large hole in various areas of activity. Thus change has to be done carefully so as not to undermine the learning environment, the attractiveness, or the income generation aspects of the activity.

Being aware of the above, the Axis Arts Centre at the time and in response to the Centre's own continuous expansion initiated, between 2012 and 2016, both an academic process of enquiry with multi-authored output, as well as a public discussion and debate around the role and value of small academically housed arts centres, with themes covered being sustainability, remit, programming and impact (Boehm et al., 2014b).

This process of expansion was thus seen to be sparking its own discourses, which supported the structural analysis for a case study. The documents related to the expansion focused on the issue of sustainable growth whilst balancing internal and external vested interests. This followed along the lines of funding, with reports to external patrons focusing on different aspects compared to reports to an internal readership.

Internally facing documentation is, in general, often aimed at internal, and often more senior, decision-makers where the premise of the value of arts centres is not a given due to the need to balance different priorities of which role of arts-centres might be just one. Thus the documents are often university-centric, focusing on the ability to represent the complex benefits of an arts centre in terms of separate university agendas, such as research, enterprise, learning, employability, impact etc. Thus, for instance, in one of the two REF, 2014s case studies of the host institution, the arts centre was central with its ability to platform a project conceptualised around the curation of new knowledge in the artistic disciplines.

These discourses – with different viewpoints and contemporary challenges – informed how the arts centre continued to develop its provision for the department AND as an arts centre. In this process, a series of local, regional and international public panel discussions represented various perspectives, leading and simultaneously guiding us towards reconceptualising a more dynamic model on which to build the Centre's sustainability, identity and be able to maximise impact.

The result of this expansion was the even tighter inclusion of students and the community, thus widening the learning community as part of the conceptualisation and thus enhancing all of the five functions of the arts centre as part of its new five seasons (see Table 13 below).

Table 13. Five Conceptualised Seasons of the Axis Arts Centre.[a]

Seasons

Axis autumn	Sept to Oct	On-site	Season of professional work housed on campus
Axis exposed	Nov to Dec	Off-site	Season of performance/projects off-site
Axis spring	Jan to March	On-site	Season of professional work housed on campus
Axis on tour	April to June	On-site	Season of work presented by MMU students externally
Axis explored	July to Aug	Off-site	Summer schools, residencies for artists/companies, CPD, showcases and projects

[a]Unpublished report, Gibson, 2012.

As the table above suggested, the Centre continued to have the autumn and spring season of professionally work housed on campus, the 'spear head' of contemporary professional work presented and which attracted most of the external income, but also the highest costs. With that, it required patronage represented through 50% ACE funding matched by 50% institutional funding. Undergraduate students engaged in these programmes as audiences, as front-of-house salaries staff, or as part of the Axis team supporting various professional functions of running an arts centre. In 2012, an introduction of an off-campus touring programme added both Axis Exposed and Axis on Tour, with its collaboration with Cheshire Rural Touring[3] and bringing contemporary live art to rural towns, and this also embedded students as audience members, artists or part of the team putting on these shows. And Axis Explored brought into the framework final year degree shows, research conferences with a performing arts practice embedded, or community outreach activities such as arts summer school or department-related continual professional development courses (CPD).

The Axis Arts Centre label allowed these activities to be seen not from a university-centric point of view of being either 'community engagement', 'outreach', 'widening participation', 'income generation' or 'employability enhancement activities' but much more holistically as a department being inherently involved in talent facilitation and place-making.

Complexity also existed in the way this is funded. Within the five seasons, there are various forms of patronage, income generation and cost contribution. Axis Spring and Axis Autumn are what Sacco would probably consider as a funding model aligned to Culture 1.0 and 1.2 that come with their own ideological straightjacket. The two professional programmes (Axis Autumn and Axis Spring), funded by both the university and the Arts Council England, exhibited characteristics of value absorption, with most funding invested being made elsewhere. This had sometimes challenging ramifications for the perception of students who, with the disappearance of a publicly funded university, might feel that

---

[3]Cheshire Rural Touring Arts, http://www.cheshireruraltouringarts.co.uk/ 14/11/2016.

a part of this funding was sourced from the income of their student fees (or, rather more aptly, student debt). The cultural offering is also a la Culture 1.0, determined by a small group of individuals who believe this is a necessary component of professional artistic development. This could be seen as similar to the belief stemming from the nineteenth century, with culture being seen as increasingly a component of human development. There were limited audiences in the professional programmes, due to pragmatic reasons such as studio capacity but also, one could suggest, due to a dominantly traditional form of live art; one that still considered the stage/black-box theatre/concert hall as the normal platform for professional live performance rather than art that moves out to where people live, as the touring programme and off-site programmes had.

All in all, this patronage model, which Sacco has coined in Culture 1.0, dominated in the last 50 years in Europe, and also here at a smaller scale in this case study in the programmes that have this patronage model. It exhibited common occurring notions of 'high brow/low brow' divides as well as the usual lack of diversity of audiences. This is, in essence, a genuine Culture 1.0 problem, and as Sacco suggests, we might simply be too hung up in our passion for Culture 1.0 to recognise this ourselves and be prepared to consider the alternative. Patronage in this case study here can be seen as a 'conservatising' factor, with a small group of curating academics deciding which works will be accessible to a public that cannot choose themselves and have a role mostly as passive audiences. This process, also increasingly interrogated and challenged, is still perceived to be the norm for the 'high art' industry, the publicly funded concert houses, museums, large scale theatres and opera houses. But this norm has drawbacks, as highlighted in the above chapters: the main one being that this type of culture is predominantly consumed by 'white, middle-class audiences'.

Being able to expand the Axis Arts Centre model with other 'seasons' that include touring work, student work and co-production and co-curation models provided more supporting structures that facilitated cultural engagements more closely aligned to Culture 3.0 whilst still mediating Culture 1.0 content.

The Axis on Tour touring programme was a good example of this, where artistic directors and community engagement leads worked with rural communities to identify which pieces of contemporary live-work might be most relevant in their particular city and town contexts. The content thus might still have had the traditional characteristics of Culture 1.0 (the artwork begins, it ends; there are the artists, here the audiences), but the curation process is co-created through communities having a voice in staging, selection, audience engaging with artists. The result is often that through the co-created choices of spaces, times and contexts, the performance is often re-mediated in ways that have the diversity and accessibility benefits of Culture 3.0.

Where Culture 3.0 models of engagement are even heightened more is when the performance pieces of work are of participatory nature. In these and other cultural projects, more often than not, there are multiple communities working together to co-curate and then co-create an event, and in true Culture 3.0 form, it might be difficult to differentiate here between the creator and the consumer, or when the work begins and when it stops.

Most of the emerging new live arts scene is keen to get audiences and participants involved and are often comfortable with co-creation models and participatory artforms. More traditionally, pre- and post-show workshops allow an audience not only to gain an insight into the research and thinking behind the practice but often they merge seamlessly with the performance. From a Culture 1.0 perspective, these activities might not even be considered a 'piece of art' and possibly 'only' considered as community arts, applied arts or participatory arts. From a Culture 3.0 perspective, these engagements are simply Culture 3.0 and valid cultural engagement with all its benefits.

It is worthwhile highlighting that agency here in this imaginary or case study can be demonstrated to being enacted in its full range from individual to collective agency, from key leading decision-makers as usual within a Culture 1.0 engagement model (curators, arts centre directors, heads of department, chairs of a committee) to a wider group of decision-makers in more co-creation and co-curation models, ones that include as describe above students, staff and community members contributing within a Culture 3.0 type of engagement process.

The latter emerged due to key agents facilitating a move towards balancing Culture 1.0 with Culture 3.0, which in itself is also represented by arts centre directors and chairs of committees that facilitated an expansion into more co-production models of cultural engagement, and in turn, made it possible for agency to be experienced by a much larger community.

It might be interesting to note that this can also be understood as a particular ideology at play within this aspect of 'agency', one that shifted the structural essence of the centre to accommodate different forms of cultural engagement. This can represent the support of 'understanding of political ideological drivers through individual agency' (Sum and Jessop, 2013, p. 219), as laid out by Jessop's CPE methodology.

3. ART, ACADEMIA AND RESEARCH: A SHORT HISTORICAL OVERVIEW

The above example of a University-Housed Arts Centre presents very well the multi-dimensional purposes that an arts centre with a diverse set of practices can have. Historically, universities first allowed predominantly music-making and music performance to be the interface between a community of scholars with its academic institutions and a surrounding community with its desire to engage as audiences with cultural activities. Historically in Britain, we can see that 'town and gown' narratives have been around as long as there were universities. The relationship in medieval times between a university and its neighbouring civil society (and later its associated industry) has often been one of tensions between what was often a closed community of scholars far removed from the buzz and hustle of a town, sometimes landowning and at times land-hungry institutions encroaching on physical spaces within and from that community. Histories of some of our well-known ancient universities refer to many of these genuine conflicts around resource needs and clashes between town and gown, originally resulting from a detachment from civil life through its association with the clergy, including language barriers with Latin being the spoken on campus, specific gowns being worn and exemptions from civil court jurisdiction differentiating itself from the town.

But there also has been a long tradition of cultural roles that universities played in their regions, sometimes underplayed in the history books or relegated to some chapter ends. Historically, specifically, music has had a long history in academia; through its early connection to religious study, it is one of the early examples of a practice-based cultural art form in academia and provided interfaces to its surrounding communities through concerts and music-making representing an early interface.

The first recorded secular professorship of music and aesthetics in Europe was that of Eduard Hanslick (1825–1904), who served as a professor from 1870 onwards at the University of Vienna. Representing the start of academic music study not linked to religious vocational use, his post included critical thinking in music, exploring that essence of what music is and how it relates to performance, culminating in a seminal book Vom Musikalisch-Schönen (On the Musically Beautiful) (1854) which often is considered the foundation of modern musical aesthetics and with it part of our corpus of music theory and analysis. Its history and its antagonism to programmatic music make it difficult to assess outside of its historical context, but even before Hanslick, music as a compositional practice within university life goes back hundreds of years. And as Jane Ginsborg writes, this history started well before the first practice-oriented music conservatoires.

Because the first universities were established so many centuries before the first conservatoires – University College, Oxford, was founded in the thirteenth century, for example, while the Royal Academy of Music was not founded until 1822 – composition has been a recognized component of a degree in music for hundreds of years. According to Richard Ede at Oxford in 1506–1507, cited by Caldwell (1986), both BMus and Dmus degrees were awarded for polyphonic composition, the details of the requirements (often a mass and an antiphon setting) sometimes being given in the candidate's supplication for the degree.

(Ginsborg, 2014, p. 79)

This differentiation between theory and practice in the early history of music in HE has had a long tail, as it is so closely linked to the perceived divide between the academic and the vocational. In the United Kingdom, possibly the Further and Higher Education Act of 1992 has meant that this tension between the perceived academic and the perceived vocational has been an ever-present spectre. That these two concepts seem separate from each other is another expression of the false dichotomy that still stems from an enlightenment view of intelligence (see Robinson, 2010).

The concept of this division of the 'vocational' from the 'academic' is based on a very specific intellectual model of the mind: that our perception of what academic study is was formed at a time when the concept of intelligence was limited to the ability to reason deductively. According to the late Ken Robinson, this is based on a series of assumptions about social structure and capacity and a very specific intellectual model of the mind. This

… was essentially the enlightenment view of intelligence. That real intelligence consists of this capacity of a certain type of deductive reasoning and a knowledge of the classics, originally. What we came to think of as academic ability. And this is deep in the gene pool of public education, that there are two type of people, academic and non-academic. Smart people and non-smart people. And the consequence of that is that

> *many brilliant people think they are not, because they*
> *are being judged against this particular view of the mind.*
>
> *(Robinson, 2010)*

But this is not only a problem for secondary education, as Robinson suggests. It has also caused a lot of confusion still to this day for the tertiary education sector, and specifically in creative degree provision.

In approximately 40 structured interviews I carried out as part of a 2006 Palatine-funded study into interdisciplinarity in HE, using music technology as a case study, an interesting insight into these tensions emerged from questions about perceptions of degrees as being mainly *practice-based* or *vocational*. The choice of one or the other was mostly decided quickly and with confidence – the associations and connotations of these terms being perceived as clear – whereas the request to define the difference of these terms often resulted in interviewees expressing difficulty in differentiating these two terms (Boehm, 2005).

The current perception of the sector is that the new universities, especially when they were still polytechnics, were predominantly vocational, teaching and 'professionally' oriented, whereas the older universities were more research and academically oriented, the term having more connotative credence than explicitly useful meaning.

But when considering the history of universities and the fact that the British university system has always exposed, with its terminologies and cultural expressions,[4] more reference to its medieval predecessors than to any Humboldtian ancestry (like most German and US universities) (see Rudy, 1984; Rüegg and Ridder-Symoens, 1992),[5] it becomes clear where this confusion between vocational and academic is rooted. The medieval university was mainly organised around the seven liberal arts, including astronomy and

---

[4]Terminology and habits such as university gowns, or the terms 'faculty', its governance, or its architecture etc. Certainly, unlike the American system, the British university system had less Humboldian ideology embedded in its educational provision.

[5]University models after Wilhelm von Humboldt were first established in Germany and France in the nineteenth century, and were based on liberal ideas about the importance of freedom, seminars and laboratories, focusing both on research and learning. By the early twentieth century, this model has become the world standard (See Rudy and Ruegg).

music theory, grammar, logic and rhetoric. As well as studying for the Master of the Arts, one could engage in further study in law, medicine and divinity. Therefore the most ancient universities in England, Scotland and Ireland have had a long tradition of a provision in what we would call today the 'vocational', with its music scholars and law and medical professions. This perception of the vocational and/or practice-based was perceived to be disrupted when polytechnics joined the same sector in 1992. The binary divide had more to do with class perceptions and the enlightenment view of the mind than with content or subject matter.

This binary divide had become even more blurred with the introduction of a higher fee cap in 2010, when, unexpected by the government which introduced tuition fees, a former polytechnic, Liverpool John Moores, was one of the first universities to announce its fees at the maximum level of £9,000. This may not have come as a welcome consequence of Browne's HE reform, but it was certainly an indication of at least one strong movement to see the practice-based, the vocational and the academic as very similar indeed to each other.

Robinson obviously saw this divide as being detrimentally influential in the secondary educational sector, but also suggested we need to scrap the perceived dichotomy between the 'academic' and the 'non-academic', the 'theoretical' and the 'practical'. 'We should see it as what it is: a Myth' (Robinson, 2010).

And one could suggest that the 1992 Act of classing all polytechnics as universities with their own degree awarding powers was an attempt to do just that, just as the introduction of the performing arts was, including dance, drama and theatre into HE also with its own HE degrees.

And this momentum carried on to conservatoires, many of which until recently needed a validating partner to provide music degrees to PhD level. As Harrison writes,

> The tension of the perceived divide between scholarship and musicianship has been brought to the fore by the progressive inclusion of conservatoire training in universities over the past six decades (...) In the UK, the Research Assessment Exercise (RAE; and its sequel the

> Research Excellence Framework, REF) fuelled the
> debate. In the EU, the discussions on shaping the
> second and third cycle forced a reconsideration of
> what conservatoires do in terms of research (AEC,
> 2010).
>
> (Harrison, 2013, p. 3)

As music, of all the arts, has had the longest history within
academia, composition has thus often been used as the first artistic
practice that challenges what is valid as research and what is not.
Already more than 80 years ago can we find explicit reference to
these considerations; 'the odd notion that an artist does not think
and a scientific enquirer does nothing else is the result of converting
a difference of tempo and emphasis into a difference in kind'
(Dewey, 1934, p. 15).

In his introduction to a collection of essays that explore research
and research education in music performance and pedagogy, Scott
Harrison writes

> Therefore, I would argue that the fact that this type of
> research is only now gaining recognition is not due to
> any flaws in its claim to research status. It has quite
> straightforward historical reasons. As I have argued
> elsewhere, after music being closely associated with
> mathematics as a university discipline in the Middle
> Ages, the recalibration of universities in the nineteenth
> century featured a somewhat contrived search for a
> position for music in science-based university environ-
> ments. This resulted in a system placing musicology
> within academia, with a focus on analysis, organology,
> and history on one hand (cf. Adler, 1885), and
> practice-based training outside academia, in conserva-
> toires, Musikhochschulen and Academies de Musique.
> A decisive moment came with Von Humboldt cement-
> ing the artificial divide between musicology and musical
> practice like an early Berlin Wall in the 1820s.
>
> (Harrison, 2013, pp. 2–3)

The Humbold'sche influence can still be seen in contemporary university life and where music and arts are positioned within it. In Germany, which followed the Humbold'sche model heavily, music practitioners until recently became effectively invisible in university academic life, with still mostly music history, instrument studies, systematic musicology and analytical and often historical performance studies being taught at university. The practice of composing and the practice of performance was relegated to Conservatoires, which in turn often did not have PhD degree awarding powers. This binary divide also still exists in other European Countries, such as Finland.

The United Kingdom, being more or additionally influenced by its long-standing traditions of a medieval university system linked to studies perceived to be of more vocational nature, such as medicine, clergy, engineering and music, influenced our UK university sector in a way that would be more supportive of creative subjects in universities being able to obtain degree-awarding powers and to be an early adopter of seeing artistic research as valid activity in academic life.

But although it was possible to study music, dance, acting and creative writing to a degree level in UK universities, and even complete predominantly practice-based PhDs in these subjects, there were still tensions between, what can be seen as the mediaeval vocational oriented university model, and the fast-expanding 'academic' Humboldt'sche model. The tension and confusion between what was seen as 'vocational' and what was seen as 'academic' were as real in the United Kingdom as it was in other European academic sectors.

Whilst the Creative Industries Task Force in Tony Blair's new 1997 government set about mapping current activity in those sectors deemed to be a part of the UK creative industries, measuring their contribution to Britain's overall economic performance and identifying policy measures that would promote their further development, the UK Council for Graduate Education explored Practice-Based Doctorates in the Creative and Performing Arts and Design (UK Council for Graduate Education) (UK Council for Graduate Education, 1997).

As the number of university courses expanded within an era that I have characterised as University 2.0, an emerging student market demanded more innovative and professionally oriented courses. Simultaneously knowledge domains expanded, and the pressure to normalise research not just for music but also for other creative subjects taught at university level increased. This included Art and Design, Dance, Drama, Theatre, Media Studies, Music Technology and many more. Simultaneously, and I would assume also supported by an increasing educated graduate base moving into the creative industries, questions of what research looked like in the creative subjects brought forward a new generation of researchers publishing on this subject. NESTA, together with ACE and Arts and Humanities Research Council, ran a project that produced a definition of Research and Development in the creative subject areas, based on the European Frascati Manual, which originally stemmed from 1963, but its 7th edition in 2015 (OECD, 2002 7th ed.) was used to expand the valid definition of R&D into arts, humanities and social sciences (Bakhshi and Lomas, 2017, pp. 1–2).

Its final report advocated for recognising R&D as a legitimate practice in the arts, humanities and social sciences, not just science and technology. It made explicit that R&D can lead to the creation of cultural and social value as well as economic value, and provided a basis on which policymakers were now able to build a framework to measure and evaluate the return on investment from all R&D, as is the case with science and technology R&D.

With it, newly formalised and justified methodologies for these enquiries were needed, ones that put the practitioner at the centre and encouraged enquiries unbound by disciplinary thoughts. A new methodology emerged that mended the gap between the vocational and the academic, or in its own terminology, provided a continuing dialogical relationship between the practice and its critical discourse. By allowing the practitioner to be a central focus, it freed itself from disciplinary divides and developed a new culture in our research community: Practice-as-Research.

4. PRACTICE-AS-RESEARCH AND ITS CREATIVE PULL

Not quite controversial anymore, but still evolving, is the emergence of Practice-as-Research methodologies, or short PaR, appearing in various visual arts, design, music and performing arts disciplines. Jane Linden, in her doctoral thesis about PaR, maps these developments from the 1970s onwards:

> 'Carol Grey identifies the 'first generation' artist researchers in Art and Design, emerging in the 1970s and 1980s, who saw the potential to develop practice 'through the process and framework of higher degrees'. As early as 1989, the UK Council for National Academic Awards (CNAA) had extended its research regulations to include 'artefacts/artworks (elements of practice) as part of a submission for higher degrees, legitimising practice and not only 'reflection on practice' as a research activity'
>
> (Grey, in Linden 2012).

The exponential rise of PaR can also be seen as a consequence of various HE policies. The Further and Higher Education Act of 1992 put the former polytechnics – with their more vocational and practice-based cultures – into the same framework as the old universities with their perceived predominantly academic provisions. The word 'perceived' is important in this context, as explored above, as they have come to be *perceived* as academic-only since the eighteenth century and were reinforced as academic by the rise of the Humboldtian model of a university, which was accepted by most European and American universities. The English and Scottish (and Irish) ancient universities have more recognisable remnants of their medieval origins may in some way also explain the British wider acceptance of the 'practice-based' in university contexts, as exemplified by music composition, drama, dance or creative writing. Whereas in the United Kingdom, composition is taught in ancient and red-brick universities; in Germany, it is still predominantly taught in conservatories and music colleges.

PaR could be defined as Linden does, using a definition derived by the HE Academy:

- *Practice as Research* = research activity in which disciplinary practice – normally arts/media/performance practice – is an integral part of the research method and outcome (in the form of documented processes and/or products) of an articulated and positioned research inquiry (Linden, 2012).

In this, it stands in opposition to the more common practice-based research:

- *Practice Based Research* = an alternative to traditional academic research. In this type of research, research methods, questions and outcomes are directly derived from and applied to issues of direct relevance to the field.

Thus PaR acknowledges the significance of a direct engagement from within the practical activity as an integral part. What is often called a dialogical relationship between the practice on the one hand and the conceptual and critical frameworks on the other is integral to PaR. In this, it does have resemblances to methodologies such as action research. Furthermore, Nelson cautions those who might easily dismiss this methodology as an easier method, suggesting that 'PaR projects require more labour and a broader range of skill to engage in a multi-mode research inquiry than more traditional research processes and, when done well, demonstrate an equivalent rigour' (Nelson, 2013, p. 9).

The dialogical nature between practice and research has a close similarity to the dialogical nature of digital innovation processes. Here the practice of developing technological tools to support creative ends is in a dynamic dialogical relationship to the artistic concepts. To resist the fashionable attractiveness of digital novelty in the 00s, early internet-based music research projects that I was involved in focussed on the concept of putting the creative premise at the forefront. We wanted to develop a conceptual framework helping to push back on 'technological push' and introduce a dialogical relationship between technology and the creative process, coining the concept of 'creative pull'. This term was explored in a whole conference in 2001 around the concepts of 'Content Integrated Research in Creative User Systems' or in short CIRCUS, and we wrote, rather cheekily around that time:

> *A major concern of CIRCUS has been the topic of*
> *'creative pull', which is our favoured method of devel-*
> *oping relevant technology for use by arts-based*

> *practitioners. Briefly 'creative pull' involves the devel-*
> *opment of relevant technology for furthering a creative*
> *practice-based project, so artists are in control and*
> *technologists derive their necessary insights from crea-*
> *tive need rather their own overheated imaginings.*
>
> (Patterson and Boehm, 2001)

This prioritisation of the creative process is key, positioning it at the centre, the heart around which all questions around tools development and choice of methods rotate. With it, the building up of a rigorous line of enquiry will have a key aim: to understand the process, the 'creative pull'. For CIRCUS, at the centre of this methodology stood the challenge of content, medium and technology (see Boehm, 2002), and this tripartite is also inherently embedded in PaR, with the creative process 'pulling' the conceptual and critical surrounding frameworks, which in turn pulls, stretches and expands the process. All of this becomes a research-led creative practice, where practice and criticality stand in a dialogical relationship with each other. In both PaR and Creative Pull, the creative practice pulls innovation and research. It is the process of a creative practice that holds the new insights that ultimately result in new knowledge; and it is the creative artefacts that represent the evidence of this line of research enquiry (See Nelson, 2013, p. 9).

Back in 2001, our concepts around creative pull helped artists to become involved in research projects and balanced creativity-driven needs with the then more predominant 'technology push'. The concepts of creative pull have more complex implications for implementation. An example from that time was the development of the newest animation features, which pulled the development of various algorithms whilst progressing on producing the film.

For me, someone who, for a long period in my career, has developed knowledge in music technology, a case study comparing PaR and Creative Pull was helpful in understanding the transference of those dialogical processes to the PaR domain (Table 14):

The reasons why this dialogical relationship between practice and theory can result in a more complex methodological process can also be understood using the example of 'creative pull' and was expressed by Patterson's phrase 'building the camera while making the film' (Patterson, in Boehm, 2002): Although critical frameworks

Table 14. Comparison between Creative Pull and Practice-As-Research.

PaR and Praxis	Creative Pull (from Boehm, 2002)
• Conceptual ideas • Theoretical framework, critical frameworks, conceptual frameworks • Practice • Artwork	• Creative aims • Theory • Tools development • Digital music/Music tech applications
• The creative producer/artist is central to the research process	• 'Integrating the creative user from the start of an application developing process, instead of or attaching him as a service or as an end user'
• Critical frameworks and the artistic process is in a dialogical relationship	• 'Providing frameworks for letting the interaction between creativity and the development of technology happen throughout all phases of project development'
• Utilising reflective documentary processes to evidence the dynamics in the development of both the critical body of knowledge and the innovation in the creative processes	• 'Providing production methodologies or business models to cope with situations in which creativity pulls the development of technology, along with the inherent dilemma best described as 'building the camera while making the film' (Patterson, in Boehm, 2002)
• PaR accepted as a valid research methodology	• 'Providing the framework in which individuals artists can participate in research projects, without the need of membership to academic institutions'

and the creative process are ideally in constant dialogue with each other, they often do not move at the same speed. Within the creative pull paradigm, if the technology advances too much, it becomes technology push; if the critical and theoretical explorations advance too far ahead, it becomes merely a brain game, not a theoretical exploration, a creative exercise in ideas only without the anchoring to an underpinning and resulting practice. Within PaR, these steps can be quite uneven. For periods of time, the creative practice might be pushing ahead, with conceptual and critical development of frameworks having to catch up in a writing-up phase. Although this is often the reality, it is not ideal, where – for instance, in a PhD process – the writing and critical research should go hand in hand in exploring the insights gained from this process in a creative process in order to gain insights about the act of creation.

This difference in the pace of development creates a number of challenges. It creates a stop-and-go process that needs to be constantly negotiated. Additionally, we creative academics can find this process hard, as our learning environments and disciplinary structures are not as often used to engaging in enquiries that include both the practical AND the theoretical simultaneously. Choosing one or the other often seems the easier way. The guidelines for writing pure written dissertations or creating only a compositional portfolio are much easier to understand, and easier to navigate, than doing both simultaneously and putting them into a meaningful dialogue with each other. However, I, like many others, would maintain that this is essential for creative, research-active academics, as this is a process aimed at bringing to light the new knowledge contained in the processes explored. A creative practice without the criticality or the development of rigorous conceptual and theoretical frameworks that expose new insights is just a creative practice, and it can live very well without an attachment to a research process.

So it is my personal opinion that creative portfolios without a substantive critical commentary do not have the ineligible right to be seen as research outputs. The explicit-making of the new insights that the dialogical relationship between theory and practice exposes is key to my definition of research, as insights need to be relatable across time and space. However, what has muddied the water and thus is still controversial in the academy is, of course, portfolio PhDs that quite a few research-intensive universities run, as well as UK Research Excellence Framework provision of allowing creative outputs to be submitted with just 300-word statements. I personally would ask what differentiates a researching artist-academic in the academy from a professional artist in the professional world, which can very well provide a 300-word statement. Innovation of – and new knowledge contained in – the practice is (or should) not be the deciding factor here, but what a researcher does is to make this new knowledge explicit. This might be through a thesis, a book, a film or a podcast, but all of these forms of using words to bring new insights into the light need an academically rigorous scaffolding, with the equivalent systems for referencing, evidencing, arguing and documenting.

Music, as it is the longest academic subject by far in our universities, has always had a more privileged position, with PhDs by composition being a common occurrence for decades, following on from D.Mus. requiring composition portfolios. And this privileged position has also allowed music to leverage the entrance of other creative art forms into the research community. It becomes clear that, apart from the subject's historical evolution within academia, there is not so much difference between a portfolio of compositions vs a portfolio of choreographed dance performances or a portfolio of creative writings or novels.

But although PhDs by Novel do exist in some universities, mostly for those subject areas within the creative arts that did not have the fortune of having a 100 + year history of music in academia, PaR is one of the few ways to consider a creative process that leads to an innovative practice as a valid a research activity. Documentation becomes even more essential in those art forms that are ephemeral and poses another challenge; how to capture the process, the artefact and the dialogue in-between?

> *The practice as research descriptor states clearly that 'outcomes' of research can be considered through 'documented processes' as well as 'products' – which suggests that the knowledge value of the research undertaking is positioned through and within the activity itself and not simply through objects/artefacts in relation to a specific field of inquiry. It is significant then to consider practice as research (...) as exactly what it declares itself to be – a distinct methodology that has fundamental regard for a close, and experientially derived, research praxis.*
>
> *(Linden, 2012)*

Thus, in its essence, PaR has the ability to close the gaps between the practice and the 'academic', and thus addresses and simultaneously elevates the formerly perceived vocational for many ephemeral performance disciplines (such as live arts, dance, songwriting, acting).

In a country such as the United Kingdom, where the creative sector has flourished in industry as well as in HE, it is no wonder that this new methodology has been welcomed with open arms.

Even beyond the performance disciplines, this explicit-making of something ephemeral is of significance, as is having a rigorous methodology that puts the 'I' right into the middle of the process, where it cannot be ignored. This practitioner-centred methodology could be seen as a rigorous method for many other disciplines where it might be of value to bring in the practitioner's insights into an enquiry.

It also seems to re-connect the more medieval ancestry of practice-oriented disciplines such as medicine and divinity, with a more contemporary research methodology that does not ignore more post-modern notions of impossible objectivity. The practitioner-researcher herself/himself is an explicit part of the methodology.

PaR thus provides a crucial solution not only for enquiries in the arts but for all knowledge enquiries where the experience of the practitioner is in a dialogical relationship with various contextual, critical and conceptual frameworks.

With that, it often opens up research and PhDs to professionals beyond the academy, those who really want to interrogate and develop their practice by allowing it to be imbricated by new lines of critical enquiry.

Tableau #5: A University-Housed Research Centre

As an example of a community of academically based artist-researchers, this tableau or case study looks at a university-housed research centre that focuses on artistic practices or research around cultural engagement. The documents that this tableau draws from are its website, REF21 documents and its first annual report (Tableau #5).

Tableau # 5. An Arts Research Centre (2021).

Tableau and CPE	An Arts Research Centre (2021)
Structural selectivity	• A university houses creatively themed research centre
Discursive	• Website and blog • Founding documents and annual reports • REF 2021 documents
Agency	
Technological	• Digital and online tools used for communication and dissemination

The C3 Centre at Staffordshire University was established in 2020, bringing together existing research groups in the university, focusing on the Creative Industries and on Creative Communities (C3 Centre, 2020). It is led by a team made up of 4 co-directors, serving a maximum of 4 years each. A new model was introduced in 2021, electing one new co-director of the four posts every year. The centre as of January 2022 has about 23 researching creatives or creative researchers listed on its website, 38 PhD students listed in its annual report, as well as more than 80 partner organisations and an additional 13 Visiting Title holders (Visiting Professor, Visiting Research Fellow, Honorary Civic Fellow and Honorary Professors).

This mix is typical of university-housed arts-based research centres, particularly exhibiting a large number of partnerships to support significant activities that are co-created and co-produced in partnership with civil society and state actors. Of the 80 partners, the large majority are SME creative and cultural, not-for-profit publicly supported organisations (48 organisations). Significantly smaller is the number of partnerships with for-profit business organisations (13), the rest being local authority, university or learning organisation partnerships. The ratio is, I would suggest, indicative of similar centres around the United Kingdom and could be interpreted in the following manner:

First, where arts in academia is used as a publicly oriented interface between what is within the university and what is outside of its walls, it is still dominated by research into types of cultural engagement of Sacco's Culture 1.0, prioritising more often a deep, innovative, individualised practice. Increasing from RAE 2008, but still in the minority are occurrences of research that is co-produced, collective and of participatory nature, conforming to Sacco's Culture 3.0 types of cultural engagements. The table below exemplifies it by depicting search terms in the titles of REF, 2014 Impact Case Studies in the United Kingdom overall (Table 15).

Table 15. Term Occurrence in REF2014 Impact Case Study Titles.[a]

	UoA34	UoA35	Total
Art	69	22	91
Music	1	57	58
Design	40	3	45
Theatre	2	15	17
Visual	10	3	13
Dance	1	11	12
Drama	–	7	7
Writing	1	5	6
Painting	4	–	4
Book	3	1	4
Public	31	19	50
Participatory	2	3	5
Community	2	7	9
Co-creation	0	1	1
Engagement	4	4	8
Centre	6	3	9

[a]Data used are from publicly available Case Studies of the 2014 Research Excellence Framework (REF, 2014).

However, over the last eight years, this has shifted considerably, with society increasingly prioritising diversity, co-creation and process over gatekeeping, individuality and artefact. Thus the occurrence of terms such as co-production and co-creation has significantly increased in university documentation, as it is seen here in the C3 Centre, where the website suggests that:

> The C3 Centre provides a structural framework for activities that reflect the search for new conceptual and critical insights into practices used by individual artists, collectives and creative thinkers who are passionate about engaging, interacting or co-creating with, local, national and global societies, cultures and communities. It focusses on those areas of Ceramics, Creative Industry and Creative Communities that make our region so impactful through its creative engagements.

It should be noted that I, as one of the four current co-directors, influenced the direction towards foregrounding our co-creative values within the process of formulating the aims and objectives of this centre. However, I would suggest it is not a coincidence that this was the formulation that was successful in the university-internal application process to become a formal centre after a few failed attempts by related academic communities. It is, I would suggest, rather a piece of evidence that these values are now shared and understood by a larger general community of academics and decision-makers, as well as the public. Example Research Themes are listed in the centre's annual report for 2021/2022 (C3 Centre et al., 2021):

- Creative Industries and Creative Communities
- Co-creation, Co-production and Co-ownership for the creative sectors
- Creative Clusters in 2nd order cities (ceramics and film)
- Artistic, innovative practices, methods and contexts for creative innovation

- Culture 3.0, Arts and Higher Education
- Immersive creative environments and audience engagement, participatory art forms
- Artistic practice as identity formation for individuals and communities

Its annual report lays out its core aims to contribute to new knowledge produced for and by 'applying creative practices at the intersections of university, industry and society' and lists that in the academic year of 2021, members of this centre have bid for projects of value to the University of £3,475,324.00 (C3 Centre et al., 2021, p. 8).

Amongst its targeted funders for project applications, it lists the following.

- Trans-Atlantic Platform for Social Sciences and Humanities (T-AP);
- Engineering and Physical Sciences Research Council (EPSRC);
- Leverhulme Trust (LT);
- UK Research and Innovation (UKRI);
- Women's Aid;
- Erasmus+ (EU);
- Arts and Humanities Research Council (AHRC);
- Royal Society of Edinburgh (RSE);
- British Academy (BA);
- Horizon Europe (EU);
- Nuffield Foundation (NF);
- National Institute of Health Research (NIHR);
- Creative Europe (EU)

How impact is developed through the use of arts and culture to support social well-being and economic growth can be seen from the list of impactful activities (anonymised):

- Academic #01's Culture 3.0 work feeds into the training of mid-career leaders and into culture-led regeneration strategies in the North Staffordshire and Cheshire East region. This work also feeds into the formation of the regional cultural compact, Stoke Creates, a key lead organisation for culture-led regeneration.

- Academic #02's work on identity, celebrity culture and contemporary society allows audiences to question its cultural and social value.
- Academic #03's research activities focus on heritage and endangered crafts and how their creative practice and academic outputs, and curated events, allow an extensive audience and communities to engage with the ideas for and threats to endangered crafts.
- Academic #04's research on culturally led regeneration of brownfields is already having an impact in the area of creativity/culture-led regeneration and social cohesion, as well as regional regeneration-related policies.
- Academic #05's Production House project is situated within the area of heritage and community participation through film and media, also involving work with and within schools.
- Academic #06's work focuses on connecting external communities with the university and influencing our own civic university agenda to allow our university to be more impactful in the region.
- Academic #07's works on process-oriented questions around Practice-as-Research (PaR), co-producing new insights through their seminar series of events, exploring the lifecycle of (PaR) project design and delivery, attracting ca 50–100 participants internationally for each event.
- Academic #08's research activities in the area of embodied practice have become part of an Erasmus + funded project, understanding what an embodied practice means to young people looking to form their own identity and present these to external communities.
- Academic #09's work on the creative film industry resulted in the forming of a new research centre.
- Academic #10s research activities are in the area of electronic dance practices, facilitating a network to support an

academic research practice in the area of electronic dance music.

- Academic #11's work as part of creative industry clusters and small island developing states continues to influence and impact regional policies regarding film and media sectors in 2nd order cities (C3 Centre et al., 2021, pp. 12–13).

These examples demonstrate that research in creatively focused research centres generally happens mainly on three dimensions. These dimensions can be described as:

- New methods, conceptual or models of an innovative, individual artistic practice itself, such as academic #02's artistic exploration that allows audiences to engage in contemporary, relevant questions. This dimension includes work such as by academics #02, #03, #08, #10.
- Critical, theoretical and conceptual work that provides new insights into existing creative and cultural phenomena relevant for policy makers, such as academic #01, #04, #06 and #11's work.
- Co-production and co-creation of research processes that provide insights into other aspects or phenomena, such as policies aimed at regeneration or community well-being, or collectively produce historical insights, such as Academic #05's work using film and media to pull an engagement with historic sites or topics. This dimension includes work by academic #01, #02, #03, #04, #05, #06, #09 and #11.
- Research about research itself, such as academic #07's work on research-led-practice, focusing on project management of these kinds of projects.

So when we consider this tableau in the context of a CPE framework that includes (1) Structural, (2) Discursive, (3) Agency and (4) Technological selectivities, we can also see that the themes explored in this research centre include ongoing discourses around PaR. This is evidence that tensions still exist, which revolve around basic questions of what

research is and what is not. In the creative disciplines, this can
be difficult to navigate in institutional settings that depend on
decision-makers understanding the complexities of this topic
with all its historical and culturally influenced nuances. And
this still can be found popping up in many of the documents
that represent various discourses around arts research in the
academy.

However, there is also a shift beginning to emerge that
moves from a Culture 1.0 type of accepted artistic research
practice to a Culture 3.0 accepted artistic research practice, as
we see terms such as co-creation, co-production, participatory, engagement, civic university agendas increase.

Individual and collective agency, here, is exhibited through
a community with common aims to support research in this
area. In the case of the C3 centre, there is an indication of
sharing the leadership via rotating co-directorships, indicating
that some centres at least desire to attend to democratic deficits in our HE institutions, suggesting a move from University 2.0 to University 3.0.

Considering how the existence and justification of research
centres draw on technological means, one can note that
centres, such as the C3 centre, rely heavily on social media
and web presence to interface with various communities. In
the annual reports, it suggests that it is 'running a comprehensive website for the centre that includes details of projects,
rolling lists of events, list of our valued partners, list of our
publications and list of short blogs' (C3 Centre et al., 2021).

5. THIRD CULTURES, OR INTERDISCIPLINARITY IN HIGHER EDUCATION

Although PaR has been welcomed in the artistic, academic communities, it often finds itself in positions needing to justify its
effectiveness. The resistance to new methodologies is common

when looking at the evolution of interdisciplinary research enquiry, and PaR is often inter- or even trans-disciplinary in its nature and thus encounters the age-old divide between those methodologies supporting theoretical enquiries and those supporting more practically oriented lines of enquiry. And as our knowledge domains grew, this left additional tensions in the choice or acceptance of research methodologies.

Universities are about acquiring and disseminating knowledge, and this is true for the arts, just the same as in other disciplines. And in the process of accumulating knowledge and considering the ever-expanding domain, gaps will appear. This may be a natural development. Sperber pointed out in 2005 that the 'current disciplinary system may be becoming brittle' (Boehm, 2005), and that we are in need of a new post-modern acceptance of fragmented but self-organising areas of knowledge, in which, as Mourad suggests, 'particular foundations would emerge in the course of the inquiry rather than be predetermined in the form of discipline-bound theories, methods, and schools of thought' (Mourad, 1997).

It seems that in the future, the classic model of the university with its departments, which tend to be largely homogenous in their disciplinary approaches, might need to be accepted as only one of many ways to support the facilitation of learning and knowledge for our contemporary society. Until recently, the *belonging* of disciplines to structures (departments, schools, institutes) often had to do with *how* we do something rather than *with what* we do. Or in other words, it has more to do with which methodologies are more similar and which ones are not.

Music technology is a great example of that within arts and creative degrees. The part of music technology represented by sound recording, music production and Tonmeister, for example was until recently more predominantly taught by colleges and conservatories. It is perceived as vocational as it is more industry-related and thus fits in with the more working practices within conservatories and music colleges. The part of music technology represented by computational musicology, music engineering, electronics and music, and audio engineering is predominantly taught in computing science and electrical engineering departments. Their practices often include collaborative work, such as software engineering and working in teams. Their research and enterprise, as well as their professional practice, are predominantly collaborative, with multiple-authored papers and teams of implementers. It often does not fit in traditional music departments, where the norm is the single author, the single manuscript and the single-authored composition as output for research. So it seems obvious that this aspect of music technology represented by electro-acoustic composition, sonic arts and electronic music is predominantly taught in music departments (See Boehm, 2007).

The tenacious perception that departments could cover the whole area of a subject domain stems from the nineteenth century. As Habermas suggested,

> *The project of modernity stems from the 18th century (age of enlightenment), aiming at developing objective science, universal morality and law, and autonomous art according to their inner logic.*
>
> *(Habermas, 1983)*

With this came the notion that we could study a subject in all its forms, that its boundaries can be clear and defined, and that there are, in fact, distinct academic/educational communities that are defined by methodologies, terminologies and belief systems. The consequences can be found in plenty of examples of music departments with faculties covering Medieval and Renaissance, Baroque, Classical, Romantic and the rest of the twentieth century. This linear view of history allowed coverage. As a side-effect, it elevated historical musicology and tended to push other areas of music studies, such as systematic musicology, ethnomusicology, acoustics, music psychology and to some extent also music theory and analysis, into the background. In this model of knowledge, everything could be subsumed into historical periods, including composition. Composition, of course, as we will see later, has had a very specific historical heritage and a privileged position in the arts within HE. The culture of learning to compose via pastiche allowed it to be seamlessly integrated into linear historical conceptualisa-tions of the discipline. The endpoint of this historical line is contemporary music as a discipline, this being understood to pre-dominantly mean composition.

For the last 20 years, this historic linear model has continually been discussed as being problematic. Our knowledge has grown beyond the ability of university departments to provide educators in all its related fields. The knowledge has become expanded, so that deep knowledge domains increasingly appear as unconnected fragments within larger subject areas. This fragmentation is what Sperber re-conceptualised as 'brittleness'.

Increasingly other models are being tested, be it through more interdisciplinary schools or research institutes. For areas of learning and research that reach 'not only over different scientific domains but also over different working and investigatory methodologies, different approaches for presentation and practice, different underlying – but implicit – justificational hypotheses, different vocabularies and terminologies, as well as different conceptual frameworks' (Boehm, 2005), there will have to be new models which can take Sperber's brittleness, or its knowledge fragmentation, into account.

In terms of research methodology, it also calls out for innovation, and this is where it is of high value to consider the movement towards PaR as an educational-cultural approach to allow particular foundations to 'emerge in the course of the inquiry rather than be predetermined in the form of discipline-bound theories, methods, and schools of thought' (Mourad, 1997).

In practice, evidence for the increasing acceptance of this concept of fragmentation, and with it less connected but deeper specialised degrees, could already be seen in the increasing numbers of degree pathways, their names pointing towards very specific nuanced provisions. In 2006, there were 62 different degree names in use in HE, with 351 occurrences in the subject area of music technology, and these within 62 institutions (Boehm, 2005).[6] And although the term 'music technology' was the most popular degree name (at 41.9%), the existence of 'music production', 'sonic arts', 'electronic music', 'recording' and 'sound engineering' already provides an example of the nuances of different sectors, contexts and communities, whereas the basic underlying skills and knowledge might be fairly similar. Everyone studies a bit of acoustics, everybody studies

---

[6]Compared to 2021, which had 418 courses in 104 providers. UCAS 2021.

twentieth-century music, and everybody studies how to handle and manipulate digital audio.

It could be seen, as I suggested back in 2007, that within the field of music technology, the various fields were moving apart in the process of becoming fragmented. Rather than seeing this as a positive process towards the 'natural' movement towards post-modern fragmentation, I – being located between the three knowledge domains of music, computer science and electrical engineering – saw this at the time as a destructive tearing apart of what I perceived to be one knowledge:

> *Rather than seeing an emergence of a new discipline, such as the history of computer science has produced, we can see a movement that is tearing the content of this interdisciplinary field into three more and more distinct disciplines with their own methodologies and terminologies. Because what else is a discipline than a social construction and, according to Fish (Fish, 1994, p. 74) 'a grab-bag of disparate elements held together by the conceptual equivalent of chicken-wire?*

> *That part of music technology represented by sound recording, music production, Tonmeister, for example is more and more predominantly taught by colleges and conservatoriums. That part of music technology repre-sented by computational musicology, music engineer-ing, electronics and music, and audio engineering is predominantly taught in computing science and electri-cal engineering departments. That part of music tech-nology represented by electro-acoustic composition, sonic arts and electronic music is predominantly taught in music departments'.*

> *(Boehm, 2007)*

Especially in England, where most BA and BSc degree courses are only three years long, in contrast to Scotland's four-year degree courses, the specialisation was a necessity in order to provide suf-ficient depth of skills and knowledge. It might be worthwhile noting that three-year courses make it difficult for interdisciplinary and multi-disciplinary degrees to be accredited by professional bodies, and it is no surprise that most accredited interdisciplinary degrees in this area are located in Scottish universities.

This relatively short period of study for BAs and MAs in England has also proven to be difficult when it has been considered in relation to the Bologna process. UK MA degrees are not accepted by other countries, which normally have the equivalent of a two-year MA degree before being able to progress to PhD study. Furthermore, it is often the case that a graduate of one subject is able to take an MA in another subject, something that would be impossible in many other countries outside the United Kingdom. In Germany, for example until quite recently, a full degree was a MA degree, which lasted about five years. The depth of study was created through the length.

Thus the arguments of depth and breadth feed into this. And considering the concept of existing fragmented areas of knowledge, it might be worthwhile to explicitly state the possibility that we do need both. In order to tackle the biggest challenges that we face (climate, energy, food safety, security, health, well-being) or simply understand the most essential aspects of human existence (creativity, happiness, knowledge, intelligence), we do need interdisciplinary approaches, and this consequentially means that we have to stop prioritising depth over breadth. The world is not disciplinary, and we will omit a large part of our continuous search for knowledge if we don't deal with the gaps in between.

It comes back to the concept of nurturing a third culture, one that is not bound to the disciplinary cultures inherent in the binary divide between arts and science. And for that, we do need some new methodologies. PaR is one of them.

The culture around PaR, including its own terminologies, ideologies and methodologies, would go beyond the two cultures proposed by C. P. Snow (Snow, 1959), and deal with a third one, as predicted by Brockman (Brockman, 1995). Both Brockman and Snow used the term 'third culture thinking', and the new PaR methodology can be seen to have emerged from this background of encountering a boundary divide and attempting to devise bridges to gap it.

However, when Brockman uses the term 'third culture', in
response to Snow, he implies that the scientific method, e.g.
empiricism, should be considered much more widely (Brockman,
1995) and that the criteria for membership of the 'real' third culture
include the acceptance of empiricism as a way of perceiving, finding
knowledge, truth and reality. 'The third culture consists of those
scientists and other thinkers in the empirical world', he says and
almost implies that the usual role of 'literary intellectuals' is one of
middlemen between science and the public.

The purpose of this 'real' third culture is thus reduced to a new
generation (of scientists) who can make themselves understood, can
talk to the public directly and can give evidence of their impact on
society. Brockman gleefully suggested that now

> ...literary intellectuals are not communicating with sci-
> entists. Scientists are communicating directly with the
> general public (...) Third culture thinkers tend to avoid
> the middleman and endeavor to express their deepest
> thoughts in a manner accessible to the intelligent
> reading public.
>
> (1995)

Leaving out for a minute the fact that the early culture of popular science literature is known to be an Anglo-American-led phenomenon, be it driven by the market, the English language or the
level of education of a reading public, Brockman saw this third
culture as a means of minding the gaps between the public and the
sciences.

Brockman 'did not get it': he really was not able, or had no drive
to make explicit what a third culture beyond the art/science divide
could really be. And how could he, as his concept was leaning
heavily on an outdated Hegelian concept itself, that of *Realphilosophie*. Translated literally as 'Real Philosophy' or 'Reality Philosophy', this denotes thinking about all phenomena within an
empiricist methodology (Hegel and Hoffmeister, 1967). But the
concept denoted something rather more similar to our modern
concept of 'applied science' or even 'applied empiricism'. Empiricism is here, however, seen to be the solution to all knowledge
acquisition. The term clearly still has credence, even in the field of

music, where the emergence of publications of books (e.g. *Empir-ical Musicology*) or journals (e.g. *Empirical Musicological Review*) demonstrated that there are many musicologists who themselves subscribe (only) to the empirical rule.

Brockman himself implied that Snow (1964) meant this kind of the third culture:

> *In a second edition of The Two Cultures, published in 1963, Snow added a new essay, in which he optimisti-cally suggested that a new culture, a 'third culture', would emerge and close the communications gap between the literary intellectuals and the scientists.*
>
> (Brockman, 1995)

But joining Snow, albeit half a century later, Gould suggested another kind of 3rd culture, and in 'The Hedgehog, the Fox and the Magister's Pox', he argues that 'the sciences and the humanities should foster mutual regard and respect instead of wrangling about supremacy' (Gould, 2003), and argues against the universal use-fulness of reductionist approaches.

What comes to mind is the number of projects at the beginning of the twenty-first century in the area of performance research. Many failed at the methodological stage, where collaborating psychologists felt clearly uncomfortable when not relying on a controlled environment as part of their research frameworks, whereas for the artist-researchers, the suggested controlled envi-ronments using reductivist approaches were perceived as lacking relevance and made it impossible for meaningful insights to be developed into the complex scenarios that music performance in a real-world require. In its complexity, it needed as much a reflective, qualitative, constructivist and non-linear approach as it may need a reductivist one.

Thielke, reviewing Gould, concluded 'that we must remember our historic humanitarian and scientific roots and that the guard-ians of intellectual culture have a responsibility to pursue truth unfettered by bias' of the two cultures (Thielke, 2004). Snow's third culture has yet to still be found, and although we have made progress on narrowing the gap, there is a big threat that within this political climate – in which state funding for arts and humanities provision in universities has all but stopped – it will come back.

I would argue that to prevent this gap from coming back and to work towards narrowing the disciplinary divide between the arts and the sciences, we need to really understand this divide, to understand what we mean by the term 'interdisciplinarity' and how we can genuinely support it in our HE systems.

Interdisciplinarity has various dimensions, from academic pedagogy, through the organisational and the political to the social.

- The academic dimension includes questions about how we facilitate interdisciplinary learning, how we support interdisciplinary enquiries, which methodologies we can justify as being valid for these enquiries and how we structure our own curricula and degrees to allow interdisciplinary subject areas to exist.

- The organisational and political dimensions include matters such as the design of university structures, policies and student income distribution models.

- The social dimension, at its heart, simply maintains that disciplines are most of all social constructs, and that without understanding this basic concept, the evolution and development of disciplines are not able to be understood.

Apart from these dimensions, it also helps to see disciplinarity as an umbrella concept with individual terms referring to various nuances. According to Stember and Seipel (Seipel, 2005; Stember, 1998, p. 341), we can differentiate between disciplinarities:

- *Intradisciplinary enquiries* involve mainly one single discipline, such as a musicologist analysing the harmonic structure of a symphony.

- *Cross-disciplinary enquiries* tend to view one discipline from the perspective of another, such as a physics laboratory approach to understanding the acoustics of a musical instrument.

- *Multidisciplinary enquiries* draw on the knowledge domains of several disciplines, providing different perspectives on one enquiry. 'In multidisciplinary analysis, each discipline makes a contribution to the overall understanding of the issue, but in a primarily additive fashion'. In this, a study of music performance can include insights derived from psychology as well as historical performance practice.

- *Transdisciplinary enquiries*, in Stember's words, are 'concerned with the unity of intellectual frameworks beyond the disciplinary perspectives'. Seipel goes on to suggest that they may deal with philosophical questions about the nature of reality or the nature of knowledge systems that transcend disciplines.

- *Interdisciplinary enquiries* require 'integration of knowledge from the disciplines being brought to bear on an issue. Disciplinary knowledge, concepts, tools, and rules of investigation are considered, contrasted, and combined in such a way that the resulting understanding is greater than simply the sum of its disciplinary parts. However, the focus on integration should not imply that the outcome of the interdisciplinary analysis will always be a neat, tidy solution in which all contradictions between the alternative disciplines are resolved. Interdisciplinary study may indeed be 'messy'. However, contradictory conclusions and accompanying tensions between disciplines may not only provide a fuller understanding, but could be seen as a healthy symptom of interdisciplinarity. Analysis which works through these tensions and contradictions between disciplinary systems of knowledge with the goal of synthesis – the creation of new knowledge – often characterizes the richest interdisciplinary work' (Seipel, 2005).

What this means for the disciplines like 'music technology' is that we have to admit to ourselves that the separation of this discipline into its three distinct boundaries (music, computer science, engineering) has more to do with *how we do* something than with *what we do*. Or, in other words, more to do with which methodologies are more similar and which ones are not. The reason for one sub-discipline, such as electro-acoustic composition, to be more accepted in music departments is not that it is 'more musical', nor that it is 'less technical'. It is that the methodologies for working,

teaching and researching in this sub-discipline are more similar to
the ones used in departments of music across the country (Boehm,
2007, p. 18).

Until quite recently, interdisciplinarity was 'the most seriously
underthought critical, pedagogical and institutional concept in the
modern academy', and I would still suggest it is true today what
Sperber suggested in 2006 Sperber, that we do not, normally,
discuss among ourselves interdisciplinarity per se. What we do is
work on issues that happen to fall across several disciplines, and,
for this, we establish collaboration (Sperber, 2005).

> *Interdisciplinarity has been said to be the modern*
> *'motherhood and apple pie' issue. That is to say,*
> *everyone, including decision-makers in higher educa-*
> *tion, recognizes that it is a Good Thing. It has*
> *'become a buzzword across many different academic*
> *subjects in recent years, but it is rarely interrogated in*
> *any great detail'.*
>
> *(Moran, 2010, p. 1)*

But providing that we accept post-modern fragmentation, and
with it the concept of University 3.0, there also needs to be a
willingness to create new novel methodologies from interdisciplinary enquiries indicate that they are needed, rather than use
'predetermined (...) form(s) of discipline-bound theories, methods
and schools of thought' (Mourad, 1997).

6. QUINTUPLE HELIX PARTNERSHIP MODELS, RESEARCH KNOWLEDGE PRODUCTION SYSTEMS AND THE REF

As research methodologies evolved to also allow creative practitioners to make use of academic research to support the development of innovative practices, research in the academy, specifically in
the arts and humanities, was also becoming more permeable, more
accessible for sectors and communities outside of the academy. This
also points towards another phenomenon in the academy: that of
universities increasingly making use of their extensive partnership
networks to benefit their learning communities. But the

formalisation of partnership models originated not in the arts or humanities, which both have had a more solitary approach to academic research traditionally.

Art here, and its creative approaches, is relevant here, as it provides intentional interfaces that allow both practice and theory, both participatory and engaging processes to be devised that can support the shaping of our future and do this collectively. Partnership models that include creative communities both within and outside of the academy are crucial for wider reach and thus bigger and more immediate impact.

This is not only important for the creative sectors but, more generally, a reflection of our society's general move towards working in partnership and making our larger institutions more accessible. Examples in HE for this can be seen in impact agendas, the increase of publications around formal partnership models, the increase in perceived value of civic universities or very specific positioning of universities into a civic and societal impactful narrative. Just two examples of this increasing movement of engaging with discourses around these concepts are various Civic University debates (Walker, 2018) or individual University's expressions or manifestos, such as for instance Lincoln University's Manifesto for the Permeable University (Lincoln University, 2020). These come from a long tradition of considering the issue of the impact of a University not only in its wider society and economy but also its regional contexts.

In modern days, more formal academic study around partnerships between academia, government, industry and civil society originated in the business-oriented disciplines. One of the classic published formal models was Etzkowitz's model of university-industry-government partnership, the triple helix (Etzkowitz, 2008), which was expanded in 2012 by Carayannis and Campbell to include the civil society, and with it universities' own civic engagements (Carayannis and Campbell, 2012b). Watson (Watson, 2009, 2011, 2014) has foregrounded this latter role; his concept of the 'engaged university' proposes that social enterprise and the not-for-profit sector should be considered within the helix model.

To address the environmental context, Carayannis (Carayannis and Campbell, 2012a) also added a 5th helix, that of the environment and place, providing a physical, real-world or place-based context. Often this 5th helix is depicted as an overarching bubble, holding all others in a place within the real world. But it is also often easier to consider the 5th helix a separate helix, besides industry, government, academia and civil society, whilst ensuring that all interactions between various helixes include interaction with the 5th environmental one.

These quadruple and quintuple partnerships are evidenced to better support sustainable innovation and knowledge production, but they will also allow innovation to happen in a non-linear, collaborative manner with overlapping processes of basic research, application and development.

In this model, research is not the sole concern of universities, and technology exploitation may be not the sole concern of industry, creating what has been called a 'socially distributed knowledge' (Gibbons, 1994) or a (Mode 3) 'Innovation Ecosystem' (Carayannis and Campbell, 2012).

Mode 1 and Mode 2 were knowledge production models put forward by Gibbons back in 1994. Gibbons conjectured that Mode 1 knowledge production was a more 'elderly linear concept of innovation', in which there is a focus on basic research 'discoveries' within a discipline, and where the main interest is derived from delivering comprehensive explanations of the world.

Mode 2 has characteristics of being inter-, trans- and multi-disciplinarity, often demanding social accountability and reflexivity. The exploitation of knowledge in this model demands participation in the knowledge production process, and the different phases of research are non-linear. For example, discovery, application and fabrication overlap. In this model, knowledge production becomes diffused throughout society, for instance, a 'socially distributed knowledge', and within this, tacit knowledge is as valid or relevant as codified knowledge. Mode 2 is seen as a natural development within a knowledge economy.

The 2012 Carayannis and Campbell expansion of the Gibbons Modes 1 and 2 to include a Mode 3 knowledge production model (see Table 16) defined it as working simultaneously across Modes 1 and 2. Adaptable to current problem contexts, it allows the co-evolution of different knowledge and innovation modes. The authors called it a 'Mode 3 Innovation Ecosystem', which allows 'GloCal' multi-level knowledge and innovation systems with local meaning but global reach. This values individual scholarly contributions less, and rather puts an emphasis on clusters and networks, which often stand in 'co-opetition', defined as a balance of both cooperation and competition (Boehm, 2016a, 2016b).

These discourses and their related methodologies have been given a new momentum with the impact agendas of the last two Research Excellence Frameworks in the United Kingdom. The last two REFs of 2014 and 2021 could be seen simultaneously as a collection of quality assessment methods that, collectively, have an inbuilt tension between, on the one hand, a more traditional, linear knowledge production culture (Mode 1 knowledge production model) and, on the other, an impact-driven, non-linear mode that values socially distributed knowledge more than discovery (Mode 2

Table 16. Gibbons and Carayannis' Modes 1,2 and 3.

Mode 1 (Gibbons, 1994)	Mode 2 (Gibbons, 1994)	Mode 3 (Carayannis, 2012, p. 48)
• Linear innovation • Discoveries within a discipline • Interested in delivering comprehensive explanations • Linear innovation model, non-linear of no major concern	• Problem-solving • Social accountability and reflexivity • Knowledge production becomes diffused throughout society • Tacit knowledge is valid	• Simultaneously and adaptive Mode 1 & 2 co-evolution • Partnership co-production and co-owning of knowledge • Balance of both cooperation and competition
Quality: Peer review *Success*: Research excellence	*Quality:* Community of practitioners *Success:* Usefulness	*Quality:* Impact on policy *Success:* Impact on society

knowledge production model). This tension points towards a shift that some authors believe is already happening, and others suggest it certainly should be. In (too) simplistically expressed terms, these tensions could be understood as the ivory tower vs the engaged university. However, at the basis of this tension stand different models for producing knowledge and with it comes the need, certainly for countries that engage in research assessment exercises, to consider how to assess the value of newly produced knowledge.

Gibbons' Mode 1 was seen to lead to knowledge production models that are usually not concerned with application or problem-solving for society, and quality is controlled through disciplinary peers or peer reviews. Success in this model is defined as quality of research, or 'research excellence', and both Watson (Watson, 2014) and Carayannis (Carayannis and Campbell, 2012b) suggested not too long ago that our western academic cultures still predominantly supported the Mode 1 knowledge production model. The REF's focus on scholarly publication and its re-branding to include the term 'research excellence' could be considered as emerging from a culture surrounding the traditional Mode 1 knowledge production systems.

Over the last two decades in Britain, this was in turn transferred to also artistic practice. Artistic output was increasingly con-ceptualised, understood and accepted as valid new knowledge and public output, examples being music composition (or practice-based) based PhDs or practice-based outputs in REF 2021 needing only a 300-word statement to make explicit the research-y-ness of the piece of work. Artistic PaR here can be seen to be feasible under a Mode 1 critical knowledge production framework. 'You conceive an artistic idea, you compose, you perform, your work influences practice' is the equivalent of 'you hypothesise, you test, you prove, you apply' in a linear conceptualised knowledge production model.

But Gibbons had already put forward a different way of pro-ducing knowledge – in which problem-solving is organised around a particular application. In its inter-, trans-, multi-disciplinary nature, it inherently demanded social accountability and reflexivity. The exploitation of knowledge in this model demands participation in the knowledge production process, and the different phases of research are non-linear, e.g. discovery, application and fabrication overlap. In this model, knowledge production becomes diffused throughout society, e.g. a 'socially distributed knowledge', and within this, tacit knowledge is as valid/relevant as codified knowledge (Gibbons, 1994, p. 3). Quality control is exercised by a community of practitioners 'that do not follow the structure of an institutional logic of academic disciplines' (Gibbons, 1994, p. 33), and success is defined in terms of efficiency/usefulness, and contribution to the overall solution of problems (Carayannis, 2012, p. 37).

Obviously, both modes currently exist simultaneously in various artistic and other academic research communities and have done so for a long time. Within academia, various terms emphasise the different nuances around the ongoing impact debate, from applied research to knowledge exchange, to definitions of research impact. However, as Watson (2011) contends, there is a succinct southern/ northern hemisphere divide in how academia tends to see itself and its role in relation to society; embedded in this is how research value is conceptualised.

As Watson suggested in his book *The engaged university: international perspectives on civic engagement* (2011), until fairly recently, academic institutions in the northern hemisphere generally could be seen to still be transitioning out of a Mode 1 trajectory, e.g. Mode 1 knowledge production is more often than not considered to still be the highest form of research, demonstrably evidenced by quality measures such as citing metrics or publication stats for a solely academic audience. This is reinforced by publicly funded research that is suggested to create a sense of entitlement (Watson 240–248). On the other hand, for universities in the southern hemisphere, civic engagement tends to generally be more of an imperative, not an optional extra. With it comes different value systems for the role of research, and a Mode 2 knowledge production model prevails (Watson, 2011, p. 248).

With Mode 3 knowledge production cultures, or a high civic engagement by universities, or a system that values research impact on society, there is an emphasis on partnerships between universities, industry, government and the civic sector (not-for-profit and voluntary sector). And they will allow innovation to happen in a non-linear, collaborative manner with overlapping processes of basic research, application and development. In this model, research is not the sole concern of universities, and technology exploitation might not be the sole concern of industry, creating what has been called a 'socially distributed knowledge' (Gibbons, 1994) or a (Mode 3) 'Innovation Ecosystem' (Carayannis and Campbell, 2012b).

The late Watson advocated this with even stronger terms, suggesting that:

> (...) in universities around the world, something extraordinary is underway. Mobilizing their human and intellectual resources, institutions of higher education are directly tackling community problems – combating poverty, improving public health, and restoring environmental quality. Brick by brick around the world, the engaged university is replacing the ivory tower.
>
> (Watson, 2011)

In the United Kingdom, these discourses and their related methodologies have been given a new momentum with the impact agendas of the last two REFs (Research Excellence Frameworks). The 2014 and 2021 REF could be seen as a collection of quality assessment methods that, collectively, have an inbuilt tension between, on the one hand, a more traditional, linear knowledge production culture – a Mode 1 knowledge production model represented by outputs – and, on the other, an impact-driven, non-linear mode that values socially-distributed knowledge more than discovery – a Mode 2 knowledge production model, represented by impact case studies. Having said this, it is notable that the weighting still prioritises outputs over impact, with the 2014 REF weighing outputs only at 20% and the 2021 REF at 25%.

Thus for a research assessment exercise, or a measurement of research excellence to include impact agendas, as the last two REFs have done, universities are afforded to shift their behaviour towards a Mode 2 or 3 knowledge production mode, and this has brought forward the need to utilise art in a way that allows these interfaces to be creatively (co-)curated. It allows arts to be utilised to make the university more permeable.

7. META-NARRATIVES, EXPANDING KNOWLEDGE DOMAINS AND ARTS AS AN INTENTIONALLY CURATED INTERFACE BETWEEN UNIVERSITY AND SOCIETY

Over the last 100 years, the arts have seen increasing momentum in – and a public appetite for – process (rather than product). With this, the twentieth century saw an increase in meta-discourses. We can see this in the appetite in documentaries of artists, in radio shows that rather talk about choices of music than discuss the music fully themselves (such as Desert island Discs), and we see these meta-discourses in the forms of – as an example – comparative discussions of best literary prizes, e.g. a discussion of best lists of lists of works complementing channels where the literary works themselves are discussed. These meta-narratives, which many could be traced back to the late twentieth century, have become so common place that they have become a commonly understood meme; like the one that fed into a comedic act of Bo Burnham's commentary on a commentary on a commentary on a performed song (Burnham, 2021). Or possibly even inherent in the intense documentary spectacle of Curtis' 2021 documentary, Can't Get You Out of My Head (Curtis, 2021), which uses an endless number of snippets of various documentaries to create a new documentary with a new narrative message and meaning, a sort of Finnegan's Wake of the documentary world.

Besides the increase of importance of narrative and focusing on processes of becoming rather than states of being, and simultaneously due to ever-expanding subject domains, curation of new knowledge has become an important part of the impact debate. It is now required as it becomes increasingly difficult for a public outside of academia to make sense of deep but fragmented areas of knowledge after they have been created. There is a renewed call for public/academia interaction where the engagement with innovation is designed into the research process, knowledge is co-produced and co-owned, and impact is built into research processes right from the start. This is where Quadruple helix system partnerships (Carayannis, 2012) provide useful project design philosophies, as do Open Innovation 2.0 with its concepts of ecosystems, mash-ups, quadruple helix partnerships, orchestration, curation and value constellations (Curley and Salmelin, 2015).

These concepts (Third Culture, Culture 3.0, Quadruple Helix Systems) can actually be understood as part of the need by society to create curated interfaces between new knowledge and society. And these curated interfaces are often intentionally designed by our universities, specifically supported by their artistic communities with projects and organisational structures; structures like university-housed arts centres can function as intentionally designed interfaces between knowledge and society.

These creative and culturally rich interfaces are often complex in their structures, often perceived as mash-ups, with various boundaries being constantly in flux, be it disciplinary boundaries, boundaries between a public and academia, multi-professional working practices, production and creation, or process and product.

Thus the intentional act of curation of these interfaces can be a sense-making creative act, and thus universities often desire a deeper understanding of the cultural relativity of arts-related practices and the roles that universities play in facilitating various cultural co-produced interfaces between arts and society.

8. OPEN INNOVATION 2.0, THE EUROPEAN INNOVATION LINK

How Culture 3.0 fits into the wider knowledge and innovation strategies can be seen in the last half-decade of EU research strategy. Being aware that Europe is lagging behind in terms of innovation, the EU Director General Salmelin in 2016 (Curley and Salmelin, 2015) had put together a funding strategy as part of the Horizon 2020 programme, attempting to resolve just this tension. The idea was to provide less support for (what he called) closed innovation schemes, and more support for 'Open Innovation 2.0' schemes, exemplified by integrated quadruple-helix partnership models, interdisciplinary enquiries, networks and ecosystems as described in the report to the European Union 'Open Innovation 2.0 – A New

Paradigm and Foundation for a Sustainable Europe'. This paradigm shift:

> ...brings together the strengths of Europe in a new way, to increase seamless co-creation of innovative products and services to match the challenges we see in our economy and society.
>
> (Curley and Salmelin, 2015)

> Open Innovation 2.0 (OI2) is a new paradigm based on principles of integrated collaboration, co-created shared value, cultivated innovation ecosystems, unleashed exponential technologies, and extraordinarily rapid adoption. We believe that innovation can be a discipline practiced by many, rather than an art mastered by few.... It is important to note that Europe is traditionally stronger in research output and weaker in innovation take-up (i.e., adoption). To improve adoption rates, the new EU Horizon 2020 programme stresses a more holistic perspective for Research, Development, and Innovation (RD&I) and this is another step in the right direction.
>
> (Curley and Salmelin, 2015)

But it addressed not only the innovation gap but also the social and economic engagement of small and medium-sized companies (SMEs) and civil society. It leaned on the work of Michael Porter and Kania and Kramer (2011), who put forward the notion of 'shared value where companies shift from optimizing short-term financial performance to optimizing both corporate performance and social conditions', thus providing an approach that considers both the industry sector and the end consumer (e.g. society) which it will always be situated within and should ideally benefit too.

> Innovation happens when a customer becomes a co-creator of value, an active subject of the innovation process, and is not merely a passive object.
>
> (Curley and Salmelin, 2015)

With this, the adoption is built into the process of building inventions and is part of the innovation process (see Figure below (Table 17)).

Similarly to what Sacco has suggested in the cultural field, Salmelin based his system on non-linear research modes that produce the co-creation of shared value and require 'an innovation model based on extensive networking and co-creative collaboration between all actors in society, spanning organizational boundaries well beyond normal licensing and collaboration schemes', and where 'sharing and the co-generation of innovation options will enable a significant competitive advantage and will help achieve broader scale innovation benefits for larger numbers of stake-holders' (Curley and Salmelin, 2015). Thus quadruple helix models feature high in his policy documents co-creating 'the future and drive structural changes far beyond the scope of what any one organization or person could do alone' (Table 18).

Table 17. Salmelin's Evolution of Innovation.[a]

	Closed Innovation	Open Innovation	Innovation Network Ecosystems
Description (Salmelin, 2015)	'Centralised, inward-looking innovation'	'Externally focused, collaborative innovation'	'Ecosystem centric, cross-organisational innovation'
Metaphor	A funnel with a linear innovation process, one-directional mainly	Mainly a funnel, but with innovation processes 'leaking' out at various points of the mainly one-directional linear innovation process	No funnel identifiable, innovation happens in all directions, a network of multi-directional innovation processes

[a]Salmelin, 2015.
Source: EU Open Innovation Strategy and Policy Group, 2013.

Table 18. Twenty Snapshots of Open Innovation 2.0.

#1: *Shared* Value and Vision	Shared value is the value created at the intersection of corporate performance and society when big problems are solved. Shared value is best achieved in the context of a shared vision.
#2: *Quadruple helix* innovation	Industry, government, academia and citizens *work together to co-create* and drive structural changes far beyond the scope of what organisations can do on their own. There is much deeper networking among all participants, including societal capital, *creative commons* and communities.
#3: *Innovation ecosystem orchestration* and management	Innovation has *moved out of the lab and into an ecosystem that crosses organisational boundaries.* Innovation networks are the driving force. An innovation network is an informal or formal grouping based on trust, shared resources, shared vision and shared value. Ecosystems are most effective when they are explicitly orchestrated and managed.
#4: Innovation *Co-creation* and engagement platforms	*Co-creation* includes all stakeholders, including citizens, users, or customers, in the development of innovative solutions. An engagement platform provides the necessary environment, including people and resources, for *co-creation.*
#5: *User Involvement,* User centricity, User experience	*The role of the user has changed from being a research object, to being a research contributor,* and on to being a co-innovator. The locus of innovation has shifted from guessing about product and service features users may want to user experience design to guarantee that features are desirable.
#6: Openness to innovation	Society's posture is attuned towards embracing innovation. At the heart of this openness is a culture that embraces the entirety of socially-transmitted behaviour, norms, patterns etc.
#7: Focus on adoption	Schrange (2004): 'Innovation is not innovators innovating, it is customers adopting'. In OI2, there is purposeful effort focused on driving adoption of innovations.

#8: Twenty-first century industrial research

Twenty-first century industrial research is characterised by visioning, inventing, validating and venturing. Successful innovation initiatives will be led by teams of boundary spanners that possess multidisciplinary skills.

#9: Sustainable intelligent living

Beyond designing for user experience, OI2 defines innovation as *co-creation* of services and solutions which add value, improve resource efficiencies, and *collectively* create a trajectory towards sustainability.

#10: Simultaneous technical and societal innovation

In OI2 there is simultaneous technical and societal innovation with changes affecting technologies, business cases, organisations, business processes, and all of society.

#11: Business model innovation

Business model innovation is about defining and designing new models for capturing business value. Osterwalder and Pigneur's (2010) business model canvas is a good tool for visualising and prototyping business models and incorporates techniques such as visual thinking, design thinking, patterns and platforms.

#12: Intersectional innovation

Breakthrough insights occur at the intersection of fields, disciplines and cultures, according to Frans Johansson. His book, *The Medici Effect*, provides numerous examples (2006). Current activities can be found at www.themedicigroup.com.

#13: Full-Spectrum innovation

Doblin's taxonomy, the 10 types of innovation, is a powerful framework for describing a full spectrum. Doblin's research showed that often the highest returns from innovation come from business model innovation, ecosystem orchestration, user experience innovation and brand innovation (Keeley et al., 2013).

#14: Innovation approaches using Mixed models

OI2 encourages an appropriate mix of disruptive, modular, incremental and architectural innovation approaches to maximise the impact of innovation. Key approaches include prototyping, experimentation and living labs.

#15: Servitization

Servitization is the delivery of a service component as an added value when providing products. This is an alternative to maximising the adoption of products. The strategy

#16: Network effects

generates sustainable revenues through annuities and helps optimise asset utilisation and longevity.

In OI2 we focus on designing for network effects where new users, players or transactions reinforce existing activities. Network effects accelerate growth in the number of users and in value creation. Networking is a socioeconomic process where people interact and share information to recognize, create and act upon business opportunities

#17: Management of innovation as a process or ccapability

OI2 recommends explicitly setting up management systems for innovation and system-atically improving innovation capability in individual organisations as well as across members of innovative ecosystems.

#18: High-Expectation Entrepreneurship

High-expectation entrepreneurship is the intersection of high ambition and disruptive technology to create growth businesses. High expectation entrepreneurs (HEEs) expect to employ 20 employees or more within five years and are a primary source of job creation.

#19: *Social innovation*

Mulgan et al. (2007) (Mulgan, 2019) define social innovation as 'innovative activities and services that are motivated by the goal of meeting a social need and that are predominantly developed and diffused through organisations whose primary purposes are social'.

#20: Intellectual and structural capital

Intellectual capital is collective knowledge, whether tacit or explicit, in an organisation or society that can be used to amplify the output of other assets, create wealth (both business and societal), and help achieve competitive advantage. Structural capital is complimentary to intellectual capital and is often codified in an organisation's processes and capabilities and is built as a firm or ecosystem evolves.

Source: EU Open Innovation Strategy and Policy Group, 2013.

The EU Open Innovation Strategy and Policy Group in 2013 provided some explanatory aspects of OI2:

2013 was the year that the Open Innovation 2.0 model above was put together, in time for the start of Europe's Eight's Research Framework Programme H2020. It was an example of an intentionally designed trajectory to incentivise co-creation and collaboration on shared value propositions. By the 9th Framework Programme Horizon Europe, co-creation and open innovation models, and with it implicitly or explicitly, Culture 3.0 concepts, were embedded fully in the latest framework enhanced by directly addressing related concepts. In the latest Horizon Europe work programme for Culture, Creative and Inclusive Society (2021–2022), various key terms are mentioned exactly in the various call briefs, from co-creation (5 times), participatory (16 times), democratic (77 times) to inclusion (32 times), open science (with more variations of the terms adding to the sum of these (European Commission, 2021)).

Considering Culture 3.0 conceptualisation of arts and culture is important here also for project design, as it is an easy concept adopting Open Innovation models to the Arts and Cultural sector, it is relevant for those involving themselves in research, knowledge production and innovation in these areas. This has implications for university-society interactions both in terms of cultural activities and knowledge production and how these are facilitated via arts in academia.

6

CONCLUSION

I recently listened to a well-known podcast that explained in simple terms how I feel at the moment. It retold a scene in a film where it started to rain squid. It mentioned how – in an extraordinary fleeting moment – the protagonist of the story experienced the soft thuds, the Dali-like looking scene of falling rubber, the never before vision of ocean creatures in the air, and then the moment passed, and life went on. Like this was not the most unusual phenomenon ever experienced. Like the moment it appeared in our existence, that moment made it normal.

It seems we humans are designed to adapt.

To conform our behaviour in the most extraordinary situations in order to cope with life. And when we see a surrealistic painting of raining squid, we are amazed and astounded, but when it happens in real life, within 5 minutes, we accept it as the new norm.

Having lived through the last extraordinary years in which much of what has happened is as unbelievable as the raining squid, a year experienced as a dystopian novel; we accepted much as the norm by the end of it.

And this essential individualistic human survival skill has helped us overcome the last couple of years, but it also poses an essential threat for humanity's survival as a collective, as we normalise the jeopardy that humankind finds itself now in, one that not only includes pandemics, but climate breakdown and unseen scales of migration and the eroding of what was once a common and universal understanding of democratic values.

And the question for me, as an academic who happens to be part of this humanity, is how we are able to speak out against the normalisation we find ourselves in at the end of a challenging year and how we contribute to shaping a future that we all collectively desire.

1. CREATIVE AND CULTURAL SECTORS BEFORE AND AFTER COVID-19

The COVID-19 crisis provides a stark contrast from what the creative sectors and industries looked like before to what remained afterwards. As I am writing this, I am keenly aware that we are still in the midst of recovery. But having lived through various lockdowns and social upheavals and crises of the pandemic, in terms of the artistic communities both within academia and outside of it, we can see simultaneously hopeful new beginnings as the sector adapts to a new normal, as well as deeply depressing aspects as we still struggle to come to terms with what this crisis and the next one around the corner means for the respective communities.

On a positive note, before the crisis:

- In 2018, the BEIS report for the Creative Industry Sector Deal listed 3.04m jobs in the UK Creative Economy.

- With a Gross Value Added (GVA) of £111.7 billion per year and it had an annual growth five times faster than the UK average.

- From 2016, this had grown by 60%, compared to the UK average of 33%.

- In terms of exports, the Creative Industries made up 12% of the total UK services export sector, and annual growth in exports of 9%, three times faster than the rest of the service exports.

- Between 2011 and 2017, Creative Economy jobs grew by 28.6, whereas the total UK job sector grew only by 9.3% in the same time.

- One in eight businesses in the United Kingdom is a creative business (BEIS, 2018).

These figures are impressive, and I still feel the need to make sure I mention them to students, to parents of students or to anyone who might not understand how vital and important the creative sectors are, even considering just the economics of this sector without even considering wider benefits.

In February 2020, DCMS suggested that 'The buoyant figures underlined the health of the creative industries sectors, which are experiencing faster growth than the rest of the UK economy' (DCMS Statistics, 2019, February). However, still with this in evidence, most recently the Education Secretary's guidance to the Office for Students was to proceed with 50% cuts to higher education (HE) creative subjects in England, stating 'These changes will help ensure that increased grant funding is directed towards high-cost provision that supports key industries and the delivery of vital public services, reflecting priorities that have emerged in the light of the coronavirus pandemic' (Williamson, 2021b).

So how did we get here to the point where all the evidence suggested that the creative economy and creative HE before the COVID crisis was one of the most resilient and growing economic sectors and choices of study, but in terms of policy, there had been still a hesitancy to invest in it as a priority before other sectors who had had, before the pandemic, also demonstrated smaller growth and less resilience, not even to speak about much less impact on well-being, placemaking and health.

And then, of course, the pandemic hit. And when live performance ended, it hit the performing arts considerably. But the experience of arts and culture was very diverse. Summarising the impact:

- Big Tech came out strong, with streaming services, such as Spotify, YouTube, TikTok etc., all reporting substantial increases in revenues

- Music Audiences, more than ever before, through laptops and smartphones, were able to access free live and recorded performances from various streaming platforms

- And those labels and record companies that had negotiated contracts with streaming platforms before the crisis hit managed to keep their revenues largely stable. Smaller and independent ones, who had not, struggled considerably.

- And overall, COVID-19 was very bad for those artists, who were almost solely reliant on income from streaming. The crises magnified the unfair remuneration inherent in the label-streaming contracts, and various campaigns for fair pay popped up (and in comes a new campaign, under hashtags #FixStreaming #BrokenRecord).

In the first year of the pandemic, Oxford Economics (Oxford Economics, 2020) reports the following data:

- Most hardest hit industries: Tourism and Creative Industries

- 2020 – 31% turnover loss compared to 2019

- GVA shortfall of £29 billion in 2020. Half of this is in London (next big hit is the South East)

- 122,000 drop in employment (despite the Coronavirus Job Retention Scheme)

- A further 287,000 job losses among self-employed workers

- 75% reported expected income fall of more than 50% (compared to 2019)

- 38% reported income falls of over 75% in 2020 (compared to 2019) (CIC, 2020).

Overall creative industries turnover losses compared to 2019

- postproduction and effects – 58%

- radio – 21%

- audio no data, but a fair proportion continued (radio) losses in broadcasts covering live events (including sports)

- music, performing and visual arts – 54%

- Music (from UK Music) – ca 50%

- Theatre – 61%

- Crafts – 53%

- Design – 58%

- Advertising – 44%

- Publishing – 40%

- Museum Galleries – 9%

- Architecture – 24%

- Games no data, but resilient (Oxford Economics, 2020).

Freelancers took a huge hit with regional differentiation, London leading by far in losses. By April 2020, 30% terminated contracts were reported, and 46% freelancers had experienced half of their freelance contracts terminated. In Audio, Broadcasting, Radio, 72% had seen a reduction in their business, 25% of contracts were suspended or cancelled. Around 4% of PAYE staff were on furlough, with a fair proportion of radio/audio being continued. Sports and live musical events were disproportionately affected with a total collapse of live music. GVA would drop by at least £3 billion compared to 5.2 billion in 2018 (UK Music) (UK Music, 2020).

It is clear that the various COVID-19-related lockdowns have been hard on many sections of the creative industries, whilst simultaneously arts and culture are continuing to experience ongoing increases in online and streaming demand. It is expected that the recovery will take at least 3–4 years to get back to 2019 levels, but the highly exploitative element in the music industry has also been uncovered, and questions asked about whether this increased demand translated into increased financial sustainability for creative artists and cultural producers.

COVID-19 demonstrated how much artists received from streaming, as there was zero income from live performance. And the awareness of how little top acts and well-known pieces of music brought in for these content producers shocked the general public. It was fast becoming aware through social media and mainstream news (*BBC News*, 2020) and perceived this as exploitative practices by large corporate interests of the labels and streaming platforms. Not long before the homicide of George Floyd in America, the Black Lives Matter and #MeToo campaigns had increased both the urgency and the profile of tackling discrimination, exclusionary practices and institutionalised racism.

All of this provided momentum to push harder towards minimising exploitative practices, raising the vision of a more inclusive society with equal access to arts and culture sectors, as well as fair pay for our cultural, creative and music producers.

The recent parliamentary enquiry into the streaming music market, looking at whether musicians are paid fairly by record labels and the likes of Spotify and Apple Music, gave a unique insight into the thinking and perspectives of chief executive leadership of those two sectors of the music industry that are arguably the most influential of where the industry had been heading before the crises, and the enquiry on the back of successful campaigns, such as #BrokenRecord #FairPay, exposed some inequalities that make this sector inherently vulnerable to its future resilience and success.

A different future is needed to sustain our creative and cultural engagements in our cities and regions. The COVID recovery could function as a reset after exposing the key vulnerabilities of the creative and cultural sector, which with both its mish-mash of commercial and civic-oriented offers for its audiences and participants had been one of the most resilient sectors in the decades before we had started to lock down our live provision.

As part of the recovery, we were able to pilot large-scale interventions such as furlough schemes, or schemes that aim to draw the public back into civic life through arts and culture. We have seen the power of arts and culture for mental health and well-being so clearly as seldom before, as the take-up of online festivals, cultural engagements and arts activities online spiralled exponentially whilst we were all locked down in our homes.

So we can hope that this is such a universal experience that when it comes to the point where the next cultural organisation, the next arts department, the next artistic programme scheme is suggested to be cut down to save money, we all know the wide-ranging consequences that cutting arts and culture would have for all of our lives, consequences that go far beyond just the experience of engaging with it. As Sacco suggested even before the pandemic:

> *Culture is not simply a large and important sector of the economy, it is a 'social software' that is badly needed to manage the complexity of contemporary societies and economies in all of its manifold implications.*
>
> (Sacco, 2014b)

2. HIGHER EDUCATION FUTURES

And within the Higher Education sector, the discourses about how we shape our collective futures are already well under way. An increasing number of professionals and academics in various disciplinary fields are already imagining and constructing alternative futures for our HE institutions. Old and new universities are increasingly beginning to (re)emphasise their civic mission (Hazelkorn, 2016; Watson, 2011; UPP Foundation, 2018), and this has gained momentum as part of a new discourse using the terms of levelling up, hinting possibly at a new kind of localism. The jury is out if 'levelling up' can be transformed into a rigorous and impactful policy, but undoubtedly universities have again been called up to attend to their regions' challenges and to help bridge the stark divide within a centralised country as we have in Britain. And although it might be implemented with the next set of excessive, spirit-draining regulatory frameworks or market instruments, through new impact, knowledge exchange and innovation performance indicators (and league tables), this move has been generally met with open arms. Many university communities, and specifically the creative academic communities up and down our country, have continually followed their desire to matter to – and interact with their communities. Those who live and breathe within university settings know that we are not set apart from – but that we are an embedded element of society. We are people belonging to our communities set in real physical places and spaces, despite all virtual technological achievements that allow us to reach further than we ever have reached before and despite internationalised performance indicators affording us to compete on global levels rather than attending to local and regional impact. But being part of our communities, and being part of our society, we also experience more or less similar challenges in our sector, from precarious employment conditions, stark salary differences between highest and lowest earners, decaying working conditions, neo-liberal managerial mindsets, democratic deficits, worker exploitation, academy whiteness and institutional exclusionary practices and racism. I emphasise this, as when we academics want to see a fairer way of working and being in academia, it should be recognised that we are actually asking for our society to change to a more inclusive, fairer, diverse, less exploitative and sustainable society. Any struggle to achieve this within universities is the same struggle that exists at a much more general level in a nation's society. For that, we need the critical underpinnings that give solid arguments and rigorous evidence to make an envisaged future a probable reality.

For our university sector, there has been a continually increasing momentum of building the critical mass of underpinning theory and practice that I see as an unrelenting trajectory towards better HE futures than we have now. There have been increasing calls for revisiting the concepts of what universities are for, what a public university should be and the reiteration of the need for societally engaged universities with an institutional and individual conscience that breaks the ivory tower concepts once and for all (Levin and Greenwood, 2016; Collini, 2012; Watson, 2014; Grant, 2021).

The implications of universities as anchors with a focus on the knowledge economy are explored in Perry and May's *Cities and the Knowledge Economy: Promise, Politics and Possibilities* (May and Perry, 2017), and important for the arts and related to the place-based narratives are discourses around the flip-flopping between centralised vs decentralised economic policies, such as my own VC's book about Cities and Regions in Crises (Jones, 2019a). New discourses are emerging that have implications for economic growth in second-order cities, such as my colleague Peter Rudge's work on creative clusters in second-order regions (Rudge, 2016, 2021). A new Routledge Handbook of Placemaking was just published in 2020 (eds., Courage et al., 2020). Various special issues of journals are dedicated to HE futures, such as PTHES special issue on Imagining the Future University (Petrovic, 2019).

The threats of not having a public university system are explored in a 2017 volume, *Death of the Public University?* (Wright and Shore, 2017). Pedagogical underpinnings are revisited and newly proposed, from students as producers (Neary and Winn, 2009; Neary, 2010), to a focus on learning environments moving away from outcome-based learning (Thomas and Brown, 2011; Davidson, 2017), to research-embedded learning as part of a cohesive discovery-based learning framework (Fung, 2017), to my own institution's Staffordshire University's Connected Communities Framework (Staffordshire University, 2017).

There are new initiatives to explore the viability of the first UK co-operative universities (Cook, 2013; Winn, 2015; Woodin, 2015; Bothwell, 2016). 'New old' models of HE are being explored, focusing back on private vs common vs public good, including alternative models such as trust universities (Boden et al., 2012; Wright et al., 2011; Wright and Shore, 2017) and also, more relevant for the creative sector, my own expressions of the role of universities in the creative economy and society (Boehm, 2014, 2016a, 2017a, 2017b, 2019a). The relationship of knowledge is explored in further discourses, with tensions still being apparent between scholars considering it as a central aspect of the institution (Barnett and Bengtsen, 2019; Barnett, 2020).

A healthy debate has emerged, and taking one single pre-pandemic snapshot in time, just in the two months of November and December 2017, there were four conferences mixing policymakers, educators and researching academics, all concerned with focusing on the role of universities in contemporary society. On November 6–7, WONKHE's Wonkfest17 took place, with the fabulous strapline 'Revenge of the Experts'. On November 9, there was the Coop College's inaugural 'Making the Co-operative

University: New Places, Spaces and Models for Learning'. The same week saw the Centre for Higher Education Futures (CHEF)'s inaugural international conference, 'The Purpose of Future Universities', in Aarhus. And in December, SRHE's annual conference in Newport had the strapline: 'Higher Education Rising to the Challenge: Balancing Expectations of Students, Society and Stakeholders'.

In the cultural discourses, new lines of enquiry are considered or connections with more historically evidenced sustainable solutions, from the value of culture as a common good (Voluntary Arts, 2020; Quinn, 2020; Holden, 2015) to a reconsideration and revisit of the role of participatory arts in society (Matarasso, 2019; Hadley and Belfiore, 2018; eds., Belfiore and Gibson, 2020). This is balanced by a current view on our recent creative industries history (eds. Cunningham and Flew, 2019; Flew, 2011; Rachel, 2019; Hesmondhalgh, 2018). And even more current, in the era of #metoo, #blm and diversity, some soul-searching of understanding the arts sector's role in attaining a more inclusive and diverse society by understanding the status quo (Brook et al., 2020; ACE, 2019; UK Music, 2020). Discourses around building our education and cultural institutions with a different mindset, foregrounding a new understanding of a devolved cultural democracy, are well on their way to influencing policy (Henley, 2016; BEIS, 2018; Mulgan, 2019; Bregman, 2020).

In terms of blended and online learning, what was before the skill and expertise of a minority of institutions and academic communities, the critical mass of online and blended learning practices has increased exponentially. That is not to say that we can equate the emergency measures of moving online to well-thought-out infrastructures and embedded pedagogies, but the number of academics and professionals with the basic skillset for blended and online learning has increased by so much that many institutions feel now much more comfortable in this blended learning space. Not having a baseline skill set in your team is simply not such a barrier anymore to developing new blended learning environments.

Institutional innovations will be what makes individual universities unique and have character, but – specifically in England – there are tensions with the countrywide policy and regulatory frameworks in which institutions were and still are required to hunt after the same performance metrics proscribed by external sources, such as TEF and REF (and probably KEF in the future) as well as various League Tables. But these externalised levers quickly become part of a perfunctory regulatory culture which can – and I would argue they do – stifle innovation as they increase the already high risk to institutions. Furthermore, this is at a time when we need to grapple with some very big societal, economic, political and environmental paradigm shifts that our HE institutions need to be part of and drive forward in a sustainable direction.

In this book, I hoped to be able to bring together thematic discourses evident in cultural and educational policy, shining a light on how our academic and creative communities use these spaces and understanding the phenomena of arts in HE as a development influenced by both cultural and educational policy trajectories.

We in these spaces constantly navigate tensions resulting from ideologically driven underpinnings related to the perceptions of who owns knowledge and who accesses it, who has the means to produce art and who consumes it. Specifically, these narratives (culture, fragmentation, institutionalism) should allow us to formulate a trajectory and make informed assumptions of future imaginaries of arts and the academy of the future.

Using the methodological underpinning frameworks of Cultural Political Economy (Sum and Jessop, 2013) and a set of particular lenses (Sacco's Culture 1.0–3.0; Boehm's University 3.0), this book attempted to bring cultural and educational discourses together to resolve some perceived frictions inherent in our academic and creative communities, tensions that have their source in seemingly opposing and competing narratives of private vs public, high-brow vs low-brow culture, access vs elitism, corpus vs content fragmentation, excellence vs access, elevation vs instrumentalism, demand vs supply and individualism vs collectivism.

Arts and culture here are very much the canaries in the coalmine. Through understanding the evolution of discourses in cultural policy, discourse trajectories allow us to discern contemporary hidden (or not so hidden) power, class, race or gender struggles. I believe the culture debate here can be used as a visible-making potion, allowing us to transfer the solutions to more general economic, educational, social and welfare-oriented policies. Thus this book hoped to provide snapshots using two new conceptualisations of Culture 3.0 and University 3.0 in order to understand how we might move policy forward.

The pandemic itself has sped up many evolving trajectories also in HE and our cultural ways of engaging with our collective and individual creativities. There is a new drive for us living here in the present to build the institutions in such a way that they bring about the reality we want for our collective futures.

I hope this book plays a small role in contributing to this trajectory.

(Cheshire, January 2022).

APPENDIX

Table of relevant policy introductions, events and discourses affecting cultural policy and education.

Policy Table 1. 1940–1997.

Year	Selectivity	Title (Shaded = Labour, Non-shaded = Conservative)	Notes, Discourses, Quotes
1940	Agency	(Winston Churchill, caretaker government)	Quote (wrongly attributed to?) Churchill, when asked to cut arts funding in favour of the war effort, he replied: 'Then what are we fighting for?'
1940	Structural	*Origin of the Arts Council.* Council for the Encouragement of Music and the Arts (CEMA).	
1945	Agency	*GENERAL ELECTION – Labour win. (Clement Attlee) (Majority 146)*	Festival of Britain – Labour cabinet member Herbert Morrison was the prime mover, associated strongly with the Labour Government. Churchill referred to the forthcoming Festival of Britain as having a Socialist agenda.
1946	Structural	Arts Council – A Royal Charter was granted on 9 August 1946	
1950	Agency	*GENERAL ELECTION – Labour win. (Clement Attlee) (Majority 5)*	
1951		*Festival of Britain* was a national exhibition and fair that reached millions of visitors throughout the United Kingdom. Included Architecture, Design, the Arts and Science.[1]	
1951	Agency	SNAP ELECTION – Conservatives win. (Winston Churchill) (Majority 17)	Churchill's first act as Prime Minister in October 1951 was to clear the South Bank Festival site.
1953	Discursive	Coronation of Elizabeth II	
1955	Agency	*GENERAL ELECTION* – Conservatives win. (Anthony Eden)	
1959	Agency	*GENERAL ELECTION* – Conservatives win. (Harold Macmillan)	

Year	Type	Description	Notes
1964	Agency	GENERAL ELECTION – Labour win. (Harold Wilson) (Maj 4)	Swinging Sixties. 'The Swinging City' (Time magazine April 1966). Flourishing art, music and fashion. Key actors: The Beatles, miniskirts, Twiggy, The Who, Kinks, Rolling Stones. Radio stations: Radio Caroline and Singing Radio England, etc.
1965	Discursive	Labour Party: A Policy for the Arts: The First Steps. A White Paper (Jenny Lee).	
1966	Agency	GENERAL ELECTION – Labour win. (Harold Wilson) (Maj 98)	
1967	Discursive	The supplemental Charter to the Arts Council of Great Britain (7th February 1967) with devolved powers to Scotland and Wales, the basis for today's Scottish Arts Council and Arts Council of Wales.	
1970	Agency	GENERAL ELECTION – Conservatives win. (Edward Heath) (majority by 30)	As Secretary of State for Education and Science in the Heath Government, Margaret Thatcher had attempted to introduce charges for entry to state museums and galleries. These policies were rejected in 1974 by the incoming Labour Government (Mulholland, 2003, p. Notes).
1970	Structural	Department of Trade and Industry created (DTI). Existed 1970–2007	
1974	Agency	General Election x2 – Labour win. (Harold Wilson) (Minority government by 33, then in same year new election: majority by 3)	
1974	Agency/Discursive	Office of Minister for the Arts (July 1974) Report on the Arts – Fruits of Patronage.	
1977	Discursive	The Arts and the People – Labour Policy towards the Arts	

Policy Table 1. (Continued)

Year	Selectivity	Title (Shaded = Labour, Non-shaded = Conservative)	Notes, Discourses, Quotes
1978	Discursive	Conservative Party: The Arts – The Way Forward	In the 1979 Arts Council report responded to the election and the Conservative manifesto, highlighting the risk if it were to lose its independence.
1979	Agency	GENERAL ELECTION – Conservatives win. *(Margaret Thatcher) (majority by 43)*	
1979	Discursive	Patronage and Responsibility. Arts Council of Great Britain – 34th annual report	Conservative Secretary of State, Mark Carlisle, took greater control of curriculum matters and oversaw the abolition of the Schools' Council and its replacement with the School Curriculum and Development Committee and the Secondary Examinations Council, the members of which were appointed by the Secretary of State. (UK Parliament, 2009). Changes in the National Curriculum in Schools altered the manner in which the arts are taught in schools (see Stephenson et al., 2000, p. 26). The arts curriculum now shifted focus on art education, much of it teacher training. This could be contextualized in the 1980s and 1990s debate of 'cultural democracy' versus the 'democratisation of culture' (Stephenson et al., 2000, p. 26), or in other words, an inherent criticism of mass culture vs a defence of intellectual culture. The Higher Education Act allowed Polytechnics and their more vocational oriented Arts offer to become universities with access to research funding in time also for the arts, and with it an increasing debate about practice-as-research.
1979	Structural	Abolition of the Schools' Council. Secretary of State oversees now new: School Curriculum and Development Committee and Secondary Exams Council	
1983	Agency	GENERAL ELECTION – Conservatives win. *(Margaret Thatcher)*	
1985	Discursive	The supplemental Charter to the Arts Council of Great Britain (31 July 1985)	
1985	Discursive	Better Schools White Paper, led by Secretary of State Keith Joseph, recommended moving towards a nationally-agreed curriculum.	
1987	Agency	GENERAL ELECTION – Conservatives win. *(Margaret Thatcher)*	
1988	Structural	Education Reform Act, bringing in the National Curriculum	
1990	Discursive	Review of the Arts Council of Great Britain (HMSO)	
1992	Agency	GENERAL ELECTION – Conservatives win. *(John Major)*	
1992	Structural	Arts Council restructures itself.	
1992	Structural	Department of National Heritage created (DNH). Existed 1992–1997.	
1992	Structural	Creation of a ministerial position for the Arts and Heritage, at cabinet level, announced in the re-organisation that occurred immediately after the 1992 election. (See Stephenson et al., 2000, p. 26)	
1992	Structural	Higher Education Act	
1992	Structural	Towards a National Arts and Media Strategy (London). National Arts and Media Strategy monitoring Group.	
1994	Structural	Arts Council of Great Britain was divided into three separate bodies for England, Scotland and Wales.	Now responsible for distributing lottery funding, which transformed the ability to fund arts organisations and increased high-quality arts initiatives. National Lottery was established in 1994.

[1]*Note:* In 2018 Prime Minister Theresa May announced that the government was planning a Festival of Great Britain and North-ern Ireland, to be held in 2022. The proposed festival, which is intended to unite the United Kingdom after Brexit, was widely criticized. …. (Wikipedia)

Policy Table 2. 1997–2010.

Year	Selectivity	Title (Shaded = Lab, Non-shaded = Cons)	Notes, Discourses, Quotes
1997	Discursive	Labour Manifesto: Because Britain Deserves Better	The manifesto and various documents produced at the time formulated centre-left market economics: its 'third way' between capitalism and socialism. Cultural policy shifts to economic policy, representing a shift from policy focusing on Culture 1.0 type of cultural engagements to Culture 2.0 types of cultural engagements.
1997	Discursive	Labour Strategy Document. Create the Future: A Strategy for Cultural Policy, Arts and the Creative Economy	The changing of the name Department of National Heritage to Department for Culture, Media and Sport is one indicator of that shift. Tony Blair establishes the Creative Industries Task Force
1997	Agency	GENERAL ELECTION – Labour (Tony Blair) (majority by 179)	(CITF), which set out to measure the economic contribution, identifying policy measures. Increasing weight on economic measures in all creative and cultural sectors.
1997	Structural	DNH renamed to DCMS.	
1997	Discursive	Creative Industries Task Force (CITF)	
1997	Discursive	Dearing Report: National Committee of Inquiry into Higher Education	Commissioned before the general election, recommended tuition fees and 7th research council for arts and humanities. Initiating of AHRB in 1998. (Dearing, 1997)
1998	Discursive	Chris Smith (Secretary of State), Creative Britain	Publication of a collected series of speeches and specially written chapters Secretary of State Chris Smith spells out the benefits of the arts to both the social and economic health of the nation and demonstrates that the nurturing and celebration of creative talent must be at the very heart of the political agenda.
1998	Discursive	A New Cultural Framework 1998 and The Creative Industries Mapping Document 1998	Identification and measures of the creative industries, employing 1.4 million people and generating an estimated £60 billion a year, 5% of total UK income
1998	Structural	Establishment of the Arts and Humanities Research Board (AHRB)	Following guidance from the Dearing Report, research and postgraduate training for arts and humanities was addressed

Policy Table 2. (Continued)

Year	Selectivity	Title (Shaded = Lab, Non-shaded = Cons)	Notes, Discourses, Quotes
			by the introduction of AHRB, not quite a research council, but on its way to becoming one.
1998	Structural/Agency	National Endowment for Science, Technology and the Arts (NESTA)	NESTA was set up by an independent endowment in the United Kingdom established by an Act of Parliament. Driver and founding chairman was David Puttnam (Film Producer of *Local Hero, Chariots of Fire, The Killing Fields, Being Human*).
2000	Structural	UK Film Council established, under DCMS.	Established to pool investment (including lottery funding) to the film industry. (Disbanded in 2011 in the bonfire of the quangos)
2001	Structural	Department of Education and Skills created	
2001	Agency	*GENERAL ELECTION* – Labour (Tony Blair) (majority by 167)	
2001	Discursive	Business Clusters in the UK: A First Assessment, Department of Trade and Industry, London.	
2002	Structural	Government (DCMS) reorganises arts funding regionally.	The arts funding system in England underwent considerable reorganisation in 2002 when all of the regional arts boards were subsumed into Arts Council England and became regional offices of the national organisation.
2002	Discursive	Government review of research funding in the arts and humanities	Recommendation for AHRB to become a full research council. (Steering Group to Education Ministers, 2002)
2003	Discursive	DCMS Strategic Framework 2003–2006	

Year	Type	Title	Description
2003	Discursive	Lambert Review of Business-University Collaboration	Concluded the biggest challenge to be demand for research in the business sectors. Biggest policy suggestion: best form of knowledge transfer comes when a talented researcher moves out of the university and into business, or vice versa (p. 12).
2003	Discursive	The Future of Higher Education	Recommendations for top-up fees. Bill was passed only in 2004 with 5 votes majority (316 ayes vs 311 noes). (DfES, 2003)
2004	Discursive	Government and the Value of Culture	Authored by Tessa Jowell, the Secretary of State for Culture, Media and Sport from 2001 to 2007, differentiating again publicly funded 'culture' and industry connected 'entertainment'. A distinction between 'culture' and 'entertainment' thus re-emerged in DCMS policy discourse. While the recommendations of Supporting Excellence in the Arts – From Measurement to Judgement (the McMaster Report) would. (Flew, 2012, p. 22)
2004	Discursive	'Micky Mouse Degrees'	The term was raised publicly by Minister of State for Universities Margaret Hodge, and the ongoing public discourse highlighted the tensions between perceived vocational and academic degrees, as well as the value differential between new universities and old universities. Creative industries and sectors were in the middle of this debate, as many of the degrees were associated with the entertainment industries, such as music, film and games. (See BBC Education News, 2003)
2005		AHRC (from AHRB)	ARHB becomes AHRC.
2005		GENERAL ELECTION – Labour (Tony Blair) (majority by 66)	
2006	Discursive	NESTA Report: Creating Growth: How the UK can develop world-class creative businesses	A report for policy makers attempting to provide an alternative model for measuring the performance of the creative industries in the United Kingdom.

Policy Table 2. (Continued)

Year	Selectivity	Title (Shaded = Lab, Non-shaded = Cons)	Notes, Discourses, Quotes
2007	Discursive	The Work Foundation, Staying Ahead: The Economic Performance of the UK's Creative Industries	A report for policy makers attempting to provide an alternative model for conceptualising the creative industries in the United Kingdom, once that took the cultural sectors into account.
2007	Discursive	Global Financial Crisis of 2007/2008	
2007	Structural	Department for Innovation, Unis and Skills	(DES + DTI = DIUS) created. Existed 2007–2009
2007	Discursive	Culture and Creativity: The next 10 years	(Education, Cities driven by creativity. lookup quote)
2008	Discursive	Creative Britain: New Talents for the New Economy	'The vision is of a Britain in ten years' time where the local economies in our biggest cities are driven by creativity' (DCMS, 2008, p. 8) Creative Industries Economic Estimates 2009 Digital Britain Implementation Plan – August 2009
2009	Structural	BIS created	Department for Business, Innovation and Skills created (DIUS + BERR = BIS). Existed 2009–2016
2009	Discursive	White paper: Higher Ambitions: the future of universities in a knowledge economy	Lead author was Lord John Browne.

Policy Table 3. 2010–2017.

Year	Selectivity	Title	Notes, Discourses, Quotes
2010	Agency	*GENERAL ELECTION* – Conservative win (David Cameron) (coalition government)	Conservatives get into government in coalition with the LibDems (David Cameron)
2010	Discursive	The Browne Report	Securing a sustainable future for higher education: an independent review of higher education funding and student finance, Lord John Browne
2010	Discursive/Agency	ACE: Great Art and Culture for Everyone: 10-year strategic framework. This 10-year framework pre-empted a new strategy that the new incoming ACE Chief Executive Darren Henley pushed forward in 2014, having been commissioned in 2011 by DCMS and DoE to undertake an independent review of the funding and delivery of music education in England. In the years before, under Labour, he was influential, having chaired a music advocacy group set up the then Education minister Andrew Adonis between 2007 and 2019. This continued in his role co-chairing with then Schools Minister Liz Truss and Ed Vaizey, the government's Cultural Education Board.	'Public Bodies Reform – Proposals for Change'. Known as 'Bonfire of the Quangos'. Following (relevant) bodies were considered for abolition or mergers: Advisory Council on Libraries, Design Council, NESTA, Museums, Libraries and Archives Council, UK Film Council, The Theatres Trust, Ofcom, National Lottery Commission, Regional Development Agencies. (DCMS, 2010) The Design Council became an independent charity, merged with the Commission for Architecture and the Built Environment (CABE). UK Film Council (established 20,000) closed on 31 March 2011, with many of its functions passing to the British Film Institute, sponsored by DCMS. NESTA (established 1998) ceased to be a non-departmental public body and became an independent registered charity. All nine regional development agencies (RDAs) were abolished, with remit given to local councils and local enterprise partnerships (LEPs) (without existing funding transferred)
2010	Govt/DCMS	Bonfire of the Quangos	
2011	Structural	The Design Council closed. UK Film Council (established 2000) closed.	
2012	Structural	NESTA (established 1998) became an independent charity. Regional development agencies (RDAs) closed. Museums, Libraries and Archives Council (MLA) closed. Museums were moved to the remit of the Arts Council England.	
2012	Discursive	London Olympics	
2013	Discursive	Nesta: A Manifesto for the Creative Economy.	

Policy Table 3. (Continued)

Year	Selectivity	Title	Notes, Discourses, Quotes
2014	Agency	Darren Henley was announced new Chief Executive of Arts Council England	Darren Henley succeeded Alan Davey as Chief Executive of the Arts Council England.
2015	Agency	GENERAL ELECTION – Conservative win (Cameron – May) (majority – 12)	
2016	Structural	Department for Business, Energy and Industrial Strategy created (BIS=>BEIS). 2016 – present.	
2016	Discursive	Nesta: The Geography of Creativity in the UK.[2] (Mateos-Garcia, J. & Bakshi, H.)	
2016	Discursive	Nesta: Cultural policy in the time of the creative industries	
2016	Discursive	The Govt DCMS The Culture White Paper	
2016	Discursive	ACE and 64 Million Artists	Report on Everyday Creativity: from Great Art and Culture for Everyone, to Great Art and Culture by, with and for Everyone.
2016	Structural	EU Referendum ('Brexit')	For the next year, public discourse would be almost solely about our relationship with the EU, including sector-specific discourses. Creative Industries largely expressed anxieties about its ability for the live, performing and touring sectors.
2017	Structural	DCMS Creative Industry Strategy	
2017	Discursive	CIF Global Talent Report (Creative Industries Federation)	
2017	Agency	GENERAL ELECTION – Conservative win (Theresa May/Boris Johnson) (minority government, majority – 5)	
2019	Agency	GENERAL ELECTION – Conservative win (Boris Johnson) (majority by 80)	

Year	Type	Description	
2017	Structural	DCMS renamed to Department for Digital, Culture, Media and Sport.[3] Increased focus on the digital sector, which is now conceptualised firmly within the creative industries	Report. Government-commissioned report by Canelo.[4]
2017	Discursive	Govt/Canelo Bazalgette: Independent Review of the Creative Industries	Industrial strategy: Building a Britain fit for the future
2017	Discursive	BIS: Creative Industries Strategy[5]	
2017	Discursive	CEBR/ACE CEBR: Contribution of the arts and culture industry to the UK economy[6]	
2017	Discursive	ACE: Exploring the role of arts and culture in the creative industries. Arts Council commissioned report.	
2019	Agency	GENERAL ELECTION – Conservative win (Boris Johnson) (majority by 80)	

---

[2] https://www.nesta.org.uk/sites/default/files/the_geography_of_creativity_in_the_uk.pdf

[3] https://www.gov.uk/government/news/change-of-name-for-dcms

[4] https://www.gov.uk/government/publications/independent-review-of-the-creative-industries

[5] https://www.gov.uk/government/news/government-unveils-industrial-strategy-to-boost-productivity-and-earning-power-of-people-across-the-uk

[6] http://www.artscouncil.org.uk/sites/default/files/download-file/Contribution_arts_culture_industry_UK_economy.pdf

REFERENCES

ACE. 2019. *Equality, Diversity and the Creative Case. A Data Report. ACE 2018 – 2019*, Manchester. Available at: https://www.artscouncil.org.uk/sites/default/files/download-file/ACE_DiversityReport_Final_03032020_0.pdf

ACE. 2020. Our strategy 2020–2030 | Arts Council England. Available at: https://www.artscouncil.org.uk/publication/our-strategy-2020-2030 [Accessed 27 January, 2020].

de Adder, M. 2019. Michael de Adder on Twitter: 'Cartoon for June 26, 2019 on #trump #BorderCrisis #BORDER #TrumpCamps #TrumpConcentrationCamps https://t.co/Gui8DHsebl'/Twitter. Twitter. Available at: https://twitter.com/deadder/status/1143931384265883650?ref_url=https%3a%2f%2fwww.latestly.com%2fworld%2fanti-trump-illustration-on-border-crisis-featuring-migrant-dead-father-daughter-goes-viral-costs-canadian-cartoonist-his-job-973821.html [Accessed August 10, 2019].

Andersson, H. and Ruoppila, S. 2011. Culture and urban space in academic research projects of Turku 2011 European Capital of Culture, *Tafter Journal*, 42 (Dec 2011 Numero Speciale). Available at: http://www.tafterjournal.it/2011/12/05/culture-and-urban-space-in-academic-research-projects-of-turku-2011-european-capital-of-culture/ [Accessed 10 September 2019].

Arts Council. 1979. *Patronage and Responsibility. Arts Council of Great Britain – Thirty-Fourth Annual Report and Accounts 1978_79.pdf*, London. Available at: https://www.artscouncil.org.uk/sites/default/files/download-file/Arts%20Council%20of%20Great%20Britain%20-%20Thirty-fourth%20annual%20report%20and%20accounts%201978_79.pdf [Accessed October 25, 2019].

Arts Professional and Romer, C. 2018. Arts council sparks controversy with 'practical guide' to cultural democracy. ArtsProfessional. Available at: https://www.artsprofessional.co.uk/news/arts-council-sparks-controversy-practical-guide-cultural-democracy [Accessed January 30 2020].

Baker, G., Bates, V.C. and Talbot, B.C. 2016. Special issue: El Sistema, *Action, Criticism and Theory for Music Education, 15*(1), 24.

Bakhshi, H. and Lomas, E. 2017. Defining R&D for the creative industries, 7.

Banksy. 2015. Dismaland exhibition. Available at: http://www.dismaland.co.uk/ [Accessed August 10 2019].

Barnett. 2020. *Philosophers on the University: Reconsidering Higher Education*, Eds R. Barnett and A. Fulford 1st ed., Cham, Springer.

Barnett, R. and Bengtsen, S.S.E. 2019. *Knowledge and the University: Re-claiming Life*, 1st ed., New York, NY, Routledge.

Barthes, R. 1977. The death of the author. In *Image, Music, Text*, pp. 142–148. London, Fontana.

Bath, N., Daubney, A., Mackrill, D. and Spruce, G. 2020. The declining place of music education in schools in England, *Children & Society, 34*(5), 443–457.

BBC Education News. 2003. 'Irresponsible' Hodge under fire. Available at: http://news.bbc.co.uk/1/hi/education/2655127.stm [Accessed August 5, 2021].

BBC News. 2020. MPs to investigate whether artists are paid fairly for streaming music. Available at: https://www.bbc.co.uk/news/entertainment-arts-54551342 [Accessed November 27, 2020].

BEIS. 2018. Creative industries sector deal. Available at: https://www.gov.uk/ government/publications/creative-industries-sector-deal

Belfiore, E. and Gibson, L. Eds. 2020. *Histories of Cultural Participation, Values and Governance*, 1st ed., London, Palgrave Macmillan.

Bennett, R. 2019. Scrap universities to end left-wing bias, says Roger Scruton (The Times). *The Times*. Available at: https://www.thetimes.co.uk/article/roger-scruton-get-rid-of-left-wing-universities-d8ww9blst [Accessed August 3, 2019].

Bertrand, M. 2021. Cultural Battles: Margaret Thatcher, the Greater London Council and the British Community Arts Movement, *Revue française de civilisation britannique, XXVI*(3). Available at: http://journals.openedition.org/rfcb/ 8435 [Accessed January 3, 2022].

BIS. 2017. Industrial strategy: Building a Britain fit for the future – GOV.UK. (Department for business energy & industrial strategy). (Generic). Available at: https://www.gov.uk/government/publications/industrial-strategy-building-a-britain-fit-for-the-future

Bloom, B.S. 1956. *Taxonomy of Educational Objectives; the Classification of Educational Goals*, 1st ed., New York, NY, Longmans Green & Co.

Boden, R., Ciancanelli, P. and Wright, S. 2012. Trust universities? Governance for post-capitalist futures, *Journal of Co-operative Studies, 45*(2), 16–24.

Boehm, C. 2014. A brittle discipline: Music technology and third culture thinking. In *Proceedings of the Sempre MET2014: Researching Music, Education, Technology: Critical Insights*, Eds E. Himonides and A. King, pp. 51–54, International Music Education Research Centre (iMerc). Available at: http://www.sempre.org.uk/conferences/past-sempre-conferences/42-researching-music-technology-in-education

Boehm, C. 2016a. Academia in culture 3.0: a crime story of death and rebirth (but also of curation, innovation and sector mash-ups), *REPERTORIO: Teatro & Dança, 19*(27), 37–48.

Boehm, C. 2009. 2084 – Brave creative world: creativity in the computer music curriculum. In *Proceedings of the International Computer Music Conference (ICMC 2009)*, pp. 129–136, Montreal, CA, The International Computer Music Association San Francisco.

Boehm, C. 2019a. Environment trumps content: university in the knowledge society. Wonkhe. Available at: https://wonkhe.com/blogs/what-is-of-value-in-our-universities/ [Accessed October 18, 2019].

Boehm, C. 2021. *European University Art-Schools as Drivers for Cultural and Economic Growth (Report for the Leverhulme Fellowship)*, Stoke-on-Trent, Turku, Aarhus, Staffordshire University.

Boehm, C. 2016a. Music industry, academia and the public. In International computer music conference 2016, p. 8. [Accessed January 1, 2016].

Boehm, C. 2002. Music technology: opportunities and challenges. In *Proceedings of the International Computer Music Conference*.

Boehm, C. 2019b. Sustaining university arts can give us the antidote to our toxic political culture. *Wonkhe.* Available at: https://wonkhe.com/blogs/sustaining-university-arts-can-give-us-the-antidote-to-our-toxic-political-culture/ [Accessed October 18, 2019].

Boehm, C. 2007. The discipline that never was: current developments in music technology in higher education in Britain, *Journal of Music, Technology & Education,* 1(1), 7–21.

Boehm, C. 2017a. The end of a Golden Era of British Music? Exploration of educational gaps in the current UK creative industry strategy. In *Innovation in Music: Performance, Production, Technology and Business,* Eds R. Hepworth-Sawyer, J. Hodgson, J. Paterson and R. Toulson, New York, NY, Taylor & Francis/Routledge.

Boehm, C. 2019c. The end of a Golden Era of British Music? Exploration of educational gaps in the current UK creative industry strategy, *Innovation in Music: Performance, Production, Technology and Business.* Available at: http://eprints.staffs.ac.uk/3185/

Boehm, C. 2005. The thing about the quotes? Music technology? degrees in Britain. In *Proceedings of the International Computer Music Conference,* New Orleans, LA, International Computer Music Association. Available at: http://eprints.staffs.ac.uk/5064/

Boehm, C. 2017b. Triple Helix partnerships for the music sector: Music industry, academia and the public. In *Innovation in Music II. KES Transactions on Innovation in Music,* pp. 128–143, Cambridge, Future Technology Press.

Boehm, C. 2017c. In *Triple Helix Partnerships for the Music Sector: Music Industry, Academia and the Public,* Eds R. Hepworth-Sawyer, KES Transactions.

Boehm, C., Linden, J. and Gibson, J. 2014a. In *Sustainability, Impact, Identity and the University Arts Centre. A Panel Discussion,* Ed ELIA, European League of Institutes of Arts.

Boehm, C., Linden, J., Gibson, J., Carver, G., Clennon, O. and Mackenzie, N. 2014b. *Community, Identity and Locality: Sustainability & Impact of University-Housed, Small-Scale Arts Centres.* A Panel Discussion, Glasgow, ELIA.

Booth, E. and Tunstall, T. 2016. *Playing for Their Lives: The Global El Sistema Movement for Social Change Through Music*, New York, NY, W. W. Norton & Company.

Bothwell, E. 2016. Plan to 'recreate public higher education' in cooperative university | THE News. *THE News*. Available at: https://www.timeshighereducation.com/news/plan-recreate-public-higher-education-cooperative-university [Accessed 22 January 2020].

Bregman, R. 2020. *Humankind: A Hopeful History*, London, Bloomsbury Publishing.

Breunion Boys. 2019. Britain come back. Available at: http://www.breunionboys.eu/ [Accessed August 10, 2019].

Brockman, J. 1995. *The Third Culture*, New York, NY, Simon & Schuster.

Brook, O., O'Brien, D. and Taylor, M. 2020. *Culture Is Bad for You: Inequality in the Cultural and Creative Industries*, Manchester University Press.

Brown, R. 2010. Markets and non-markets. In *Higher Education and the Market*, New York, NY, Routledge.

Brown, R. 2018. *Public Lecture: Neoliberalism, Marketisation and Higher Education*, London, University of West London. Available at: https://www.youtube.com/watch?v=oAg1CVuKAxE [Accessed September 23, 2021].

Brown, R. 2017. *The Inequality Crisis*, Bristol, Policy Press.

Brown, R. 2015. *The Marketisation of Higher Education: Issues and Ironies*. New Vistas. London, University of West London. Available at: https://repository.uwl.ac.uk/id/eprint/3065/1/The%20marketisation%20of%20Higher%20education.pdf

Brown, R. and Carasso, H. 2013. *Everything for sale?: The Marketisation of UK Higher Education. Research into Higher Education*, Milton Park, Abingdon, Oxon and New York, NY, Routledge.

Burnham, B. 2021. Bo Burnham: Inside | Netflix. Available at: https://www.netflix.com/gb/title/81289483 [Accessed June 8, 2021].

C3 Centre. 2020. *The C3 Centre: Creative Industries and Creative Communities | Researchers, Innovators, Artists and Creative Thinkers Passionate about Local, National and Global societies, Cultures and Communities*, Staffordshire

University. Available at: http://blogs.staffs.ac.uk/c3centre/ [Accessed December 30, 2021].

C3 Centre, Boehm, C. and Reynolds, J. 2021. *The C3 Centre: Creative Industries and Creative Communities. Annual Activity and Scope Report*, Stoke-on-Trent, Staffordshire University.

Carayannis, E.G. 2012. *Sustainable Policy Applications for Social Ecology and Development*, Book, Whole, Hershey, PA, Information Science Reference.

Carayannis, E. and Campbell, D. 2012a. Triple Helix, Quadruple Helix and Quintuple Helix and how do knowledge, innovation and the environment relate to each other? *International Journal of Social Ecology and Sustainable Development*, 1, 41–69.

Carayannis, E.G. and Campbell, D.F.J. 2012b. *Mode 3 Knowledge Production in Quadruple Helix Innovation systems: 21st-Century Democracy, Innovation, and Entrepreneurship for Development*, New York, NY and London, Springer.

Carver, G. 2014. *Arts Centres embedded in HEIs with cognate departments. Cultural enterprise: values, drivers and structures.* Leibnitz (Unpublished Presentation).

Castelow, E. n.d. The coronation of Queen Elizabeth II on 2nd June 1953. Historic UK. Available at: https://www.historic-uk.com/HistoryUK/HistoryofBritain/The-Coronation-1953/ [Accessed January 2, 2022].

CIC. 2020. The UK creative industries – CIC Infographics Feb 2020. Available at: https://www.thecreativeindustries.co.uk/resources/infographics [Accessed January 19, 2021].

Collini, S. 2012. *What are Universities for?* London and New York, NY, Penguin.

Cook, D. 2013. Report. *Realising the Co-operative University. A Consultancy Report for the Co-operative College.*

Courage, C., Borrup, T., Jackson, M.R., Legge, K., Mckeown, A., Platt, L. and Schupbach, J. Eds. 2020. *The Routledge Handbook of Placemaking*, 1st ed., London and New York, NY, Routledge.

CPC. 1978. *The Arts: The Way Forward, A Conservative Discussion Paper (Conservative Political Centre)*, London, Conservative Political Centre.

Creative Industries Council. 2017. News: Creative industries add £87.4bn to UK economy. Available at: http://www.thecreativeindustries.co.uk/uk-creative-overview/news-and-views/news-creative-industries-add-%C2%A3874bn-to-uk-economy#

Cunningham, S. and Flew, T. Eds. 2019. *A Research Agenda for Creative Industries*. Northampton, MA, Edward Elgar Publishing Ltd.

Curley, M. and Salmelin, B. 2015. Report. *Open Innovation 2.0: A New Paradigm.*

Curtis, A. 2021. Can't get you out of my head. Available at: https://www.bbc.co.uk/iplayer/episodes/p093wp6h/cant-get-you-out-of-my-head [Accessed June 8, 2021].

Davidson, C.N. 2017. *The New Education: How to Revolutionize the University to Prepare students for a World in Flux*, 1st ed., New York, NY, Basic Books.

DCMS. 2008. *Creative Britain: New talents for the new economy*, London. Available at: https://web.archive.org/web/20080727011552if_/http://www.culture.gov.uk/images/publications/CEPFeb2008.pdf [Accessed October 17, 2019].

DCMS. 2001. Creative industries mapping document. Available at: https://web.archive.org/web/20081201135211/http://www.culture.gov.uk/reference_library/publications/4632.aspx

DCMS. 2019. DCMS Sectors Economic Estimates. [Online]. 2019. *GOV.UK*. Available at: https://www.gov.uk/government/collections/dcms-sectors-economic-estimates [Accessed October 23, 2019].

DCMS. 2010. *Public bodies reform – Proposals for change*, London. Available at: https://web.archive.org/web/20120405164059if_/; http://www.direct.gov.uk/prod_consum_dg/groups/dg_digitalassets/@dg/@en/documents/digitalasset/dg_191543.pdf [Accessed October 25, 2019].

Dearing, R. 1997. *The Dearing Report. House of Lords Select Committee on Science and Technology, Report of the National Committee of Inquiry into Higher Education (London, 1997).*

Dewey, J. 1934. *Art as Experience*, 1958th Ed., New York, NY, Capricorn Books.

DfE and Hinds, D. 2019. Education secretary calls for an end to low value degrees. GOV.UK. Available at: https://www.gov.uk/government/news/education-secretary-calls-for-an-end-to-low-value-degrees [Accessed September 23, 2021].

DfE and Williamson, G. 2021. *Education Secretary Speech at Universities UK Annual Conference.* GOV.UK. Available at: https://www.gov.uk/government/speeches/education-secretary-speech-at-universities-uk-annual-conference [Accessed September 23, 2021].

DfES. 2003. *White Paper: The Future of Higher Education, chaired by Charles Clarke, MP (Department for Education and Skills)*, London. Available at: http://www.educationengland.org.uk/documents/pdfs/2003-white-paper-higher-ed.pdf [Accessed February 28, 2019].

Duffy, S. 2019. Stella Duffy: 'Here's why we need to stop'empowering people – Visionary Arts Organisation. *Visionary Arts.* Available at: https://visionaryarts.org.uk/stella-duffy-heres-why-we-need-to-stop-empowering-people/ [Accessed July 27, 2020].

Etzkowitz, H. 2008. *The Triple Helix: University-Industry-Government Innovation in Action*, New York, NY, Routledge. Available at: http://www.loc.gov/catdir/toc/ecip081/2007040853.html

European Commission. 2021. Horizon Europe work programme 2021–2022 adopted. Available at: https://ec.europa.eu/defence-industry-space/horizon-europe-work-programme-2021-2022-adopted-2021-06-29_en [Accessed December 28, 2021].

Fish, S.E. 1994. *There's No Such Thing as Free speech, and It's a Good Thing, Too*, New York, NY, Oxford University Press. Available at: http://www.loc.gov/catdir/enhancements/fy0640/93015347-d.html; http://www.loc.gov/catdir/enhancements/fy0726/93015347-b.html

Flew, T. 2012. Origins of creative industries policy. In *The Creative Industries: Culture and Policy*, pp. 9–32, London, SAGE Publications Ltd. Available at: https://sk.sagepub.com/books/the-creative-industries/n2.xml [Accessed December 28, 2019].

Flew, T. 2011. *The Creative Industries: Culture and Policy*, 1st ed., Thousand Oaks, CA, SAGE Publications Ltd.

Friedman, S.S. 1984. *The Oberammergau Passion Play: A Lance against Civilization*, Carbondale, Southern Illinois University Press. Available at: http://books.google.com/books?id=NhtcAAAAMAAJ [Accessed October 18, 2019].

Fung, D. 2017. *A Connected Curriculum for Higher Education. Spotlights*, 1st ed., London, UCL Press.

Garnham, N. 2005. From cultural to creative industries: An analysis of the implications of the "creative industries" approach to arts and media policy making in the United Kingdom, *International Journal of Cultural Policy*, 11(1), 15–29.

Gasser Ali. 2019. Refugees as royals: The striking new photo series repainting history. Available at: https://scenearabia.com/Culture/Refugees-as-Royals-Repainting-History-Romanian-Photographer-Horia-Manolache-Photo-Series [Accessed August 10, 2019].

Gibson, J. 2012. *Axis Arts Centre Annual Report 2012*, Crewe, MMU Cheshire. Unpublished Report

Gibbons, M. 1994. *The New Production of Knowledge: The Dynamics of Science and Research in Contemporary Societies*, London and Thousand Oaks, CA, SAGE Publications. Available at: http://www.loc.gov/catdir/enhancements/fy0656/94066859-d.html; http://www.loc.gov/catdir/enhancements/fy0656/94066859-t.html

Gibson, J. 2014. *The Influence of Customer Capital on Organisational Change at an Academically Housed Arts Centre* (Unpublished MA Dissertation).

Giddens, A. 1998. *The Third Way: The Renewal of Social Democracy*, 1st ed., Malden, MA, Polity.

Ginsborg, J. 2014. Research skills in practice: Learning and teaching practice-based research at RNCM. In *Research and Research Education in Music Performance and Pedagogy. Landscapes: The Arts, Aesthetics, and Education*, Ed S.D. Harrison, pp. 77–89, Dordrecht, Springer Netherlands. doi: 10.1007/978-94-007-7435-3_6 [Accessed August 4, 2019].

Gould, S.J. 2003. *The Hedgehog, the Fox, and the Magister's Pox : Mending the Gap Between Science and the Humanities*, New York, Harmony Books.

Grant, J. 2021. *The New Power University: The Social Purpose of Higher Education in the 21st Century*, 1st ed., London, Pearson Education.

Habermas, J. 1983. Modernity–An incomplete project. In *The Anti-aesthetic: Essays on Postmodern Culture*, Ed H. Foster, pp. 3–15, Port Townsend, WA, Bay Press.

Hadley, S. 2018. Cultural democracy. Steven Hadley. Available at: https://cpb-eu-w2.wpmucdn.com/blogs.bristol.ac.uk/dist/d/345/files/2018/06/Steven-Hadley-12faykt.pdf [Accessed January 30, 2020].

Hadley, S. and Belfiore, E. 2018. Cultural democracy and cultural policy, *Cultural Trends*, 27(3), 218–223.

Hanslick, E. 2020/1854. *Vom Musikalisch-Schönen*. Frankfurt a.M.: Outlook Verlag.

Harrison, S.D. 2013. *Google-Books-ID: WgXFBAAAQBAJ. Research and Research Education in Music Performance and Pedagogy*, Berlin: Springer Science & Business Media.

Hazelkorn, E. 2016. *The Civic University: The Policy and Leadership Challenges*, Cheltenham, Edward Elgar.

Heart of Glass and Battersea Arts Centre. 2021. *Considering co-creation*, London. Available at: https://www.artscouncil.org.uk/sites/default/files/download-file/ConsideringCo-Creation.pdf [Accessed September 7, 2021].

Hegel, G.W.F. and Hoffmeister, J. 1967. *Jenaer Realphilosophie*, Hamburg, F. Meiner.

Henley, D. 2016. *The Arts Dividend: Why Investment in Culture Pays*, London, Elliott and Thompson Limited.

Hesmondhalgh, D. 2018. *The Cultural Industries*, 4th ed., Thousand Oaks, CA, SAGE Publications Ltd.

Hesmondhalgh, D. and Pratt, A.C. 2005. Cultural industries and cultural policy, *International Journal of Cultural Policy*, 11(1), 1–13.

Hetherington, S. 2014. *The Rationales of New Labour's Cultural Policy 1997–2001*, University of Birmingham. Available at: https://core.ac.uk/download/pdf/20535702.pdf [Accessed December 27, 2019].

Hewison, R. 1995. *Culture and Consensus: England, Art and Politics since 1940*, London, Methuen Publishing Ltd.

Historic England and Hughes, N 2021. The story of the festival of Britain. *The Historic England Blog*. Available at: https://heritagecalling.com/2021/05/03/the-story-of-the-festival-of-britain/ [Accessed January 3, 2022].

Historic UK and Johnson, B. 2016. The Festival of Britain 1951. Historic UK. Available at: https://www.historic-uk.com/HistoryUK/HistoryofBritain/The-Festival-of-Britain-1951/ [Accessed August 3, 2021].

Holden, J. 2015. The ecology of culture. p. 43.

Jeffers, A. 2017. In *Culture, Democracy and the Right to Make Art: The British Community Arts Movement*, Ed G. Moriarty, London and New York, NY, Bloomsbury Methuen Drama.

Jessop, B. 2009. Cultural political economy and critical policy studies (CPS 2009), *Critical Policy Studies*. Available at: https://www.researchgate.net/publication/233302056_Cultural_Political_Economy_and_Critical_Policy_Studies [Accessed January 21, 2020].

Johansson, F. 2006. *Medici Effect: What You Can Learn from Elephants and Epidemics*, First Trade Paper edition., Boston, MA, Harvard Business Review Press.

Jones, M. 2019a. *Cities and Regions in Crisis: The Political Economy of Subnational Economic Development*, Cheltenham, Edward Elgar.

Jones, M. 2019b. The Festival of Britain (1951) beyond London, *Mémoire(s), identité(s), marginalité(s) dans le monde occidental contemporain, Cahiers du MIMMOC*. 20. Available at: https://journals.openedition.org/mimmoc/3625 [Accessed August 3, 2021].

Kania, J. and Kramer, M. 2011. Collective Impact (SSIR). Large-scale social change requires broad cross-sector coordination, yet the social sector remains focused on the isolated intervention of individual organizations. Stanford Social Innovation Review. [Online]. *Winter*. Available at: https://ssir.org/articles/entry/collective_impact [Accessed February 11, 2020].

Keeley, L., Walters, H., Pikkel, R. and Quinn, B. 2013. *Ten Types of Innovation: The Discipline of Building Breakthroughs*, Hoboken, NJ, John Wiley & Sons.

Kelly, O. and Shelton Trust for Community Arts. 1986. *Culture and Democracy: The Manifesto*, London, Comedia. Available at: http://capitadiscovery.co.uk/dmu/items/84446 [Accessed January 3, 2022].

Koenig, P. 1998. Creative industries: The cool economy; Is Chris Smith more vital than, *The Independent*. Available at: http://www.independent.co.uk/news/business/creative-industries-the-cool-economy-is-chris-smith-more-vital-than-gordon-brown-1144798.html [Accessed December 30, 2019].

Labour Party. 1965. *A Policy for the Arts: The First Steps*, A White Paper (Labour Party). Available at: https://action.labour.org.uk/page/-/blog%20images/policy_for_the_arts.pdf [Accessed October 21, 2019].

Labour Party. 1997. 1997 Labour Party Manifesto – New Labour Because Britain Deserves Better. Available at: http://www.labour-party.org.uk/manifestos/1997/1997-labour-manifesto.shtml Accessed December 30, 2019].

Levin, M. and Greenwood, D.J. 2016a. *Creating a New Public University and Reviving Democracy: Action Research in Higher Education. Higher Education in Critical Perspective: Practices and Policies*, New York, NY, Berghahn Books.

Lincoln University. 2020. *The Permeable University. The purpose of universities in the 21st Century: A Manifesto*, Lincoln, Lincoln University. Available at: https://cpb-eu-w2.wpmucdn.com/blogs.lincoln.ac.uk/dist/9/8300/files/2019/11/J22424_UNIL_21st-Century-Lab_Publication_Web-Version.pdf [Accessed June 9, 2021].

Linden, J. 2012. The Monster in our Midst: The materialisation of practice as research in the British Academy. Unpublished PhD thesis.

Linden, J. and Mackenzie, N. 2009. Curating Knowledge – A discursive platform that aims to highlight the links between research activity and contemporary arts practices, and takes into account the different relationships the public can have with them. Available at: https://e-space.mmu.ac.uk/618322/ [Accessed July 29, 2021].

Mason, J. 2017. *Qualitative Researching*, 3rd ed., Thousand Oaks, CA, SAGE Publications Ltd.

Matarasso, F. 2019. *A Restless Art*, London, Calouste Gulbenkian Foundation, UK Branch. Available at: https://arestlessart.files.wordpress.com/2019/03/2019-a-restless-art.pdf [Accessed September 7, 2020].

May, T. author and Perry, B. author. 2017. *Cities and the Knowledge Economy: Promises, Politics and Possibilities*, 1st Ed, London, Routledge.

McConnell, M. 2016. *The Long Game: A Memoir*, New York, NY, Sentinel.

Mcguigan, J. 2004. *Rethinking Cultural Policy* Maidenhead, New York, NY, Open University Press/McGraw Hill.

Merola, M.V., Jorritsma, M.J., Borkai, M.Z., Ross, M.F., Pinto, M.C.V., Ridouani, M.M. and Edreva, M.M. 2019a. EUR 29797 EN. In *ANNEX A: The Cultural and Creative Cities Monitor Methodology in Ten steps*. The Cultural and Creative Cities Monitor. Luxembourg, Publications Office of the European Union. Available at: https://composite-indicators.jrc.ec.europa.eu/cultural-creative-cities-monitor/cultural-creative-cities/docs-and-data

Merola, M.V., Jorritsma, M.J., Borkai, M.Z., Ross, M.F., Pinto, M.C.V., Ridouani, M.M. and Edreva, M.M. 2019b. EUR 29797 EN. In *The Cultural and Creative Cities Monitor*, Publications Office of the European Union, Luxembourg. Available at: https://composite-indicators.jrc.ec.europa.eu/cultural-creative-cities-monitor/cultural-creative-cities/docs-and-data

Merrym'n. 2017. Merrym'n – Cable Cars in Festival Park (feat. The Trent Vale Poet). Available at: https://www.youtube.com/watch?v=CqJa-8Lz5rw [Accessed August 10, 2019].

MGG. 1994. *Die Musik in Geschichte und Gegenwart*. 2 neubearbeitete. Kassel. New York, NY, Bärenreiter.

Millward (OfS), C. 2019. Civic university agreements: exploring synergies with Office for Students access and participation regulation and funding. Available at: https://www.officeforstudents.org.uk/media/52a8d9e2-442d-46c8-a947-955adac7089e/cuc-conference-access-and-participation-and-civic-university-agreements.pdf

Monbiot, G. 2016. *How Did We Get into This Mess?: Politics, Equality, Nature*, London and Brooklyn, NY, Verso. Available at: http://Coverimage9781784783624.jpg

Moran, J. 2010. *Interdisciplinarity*, 2nd Ed., London and New York, NY, Routledge.

MÖRAT. 2016. The 10 best UK punk bands from 1982, *Louder Sound Magazine*. Available at: https://www.loudersound.com/features/the-10-best-uk-punk-bands-from-1982 [Accessed July 27, 2021].

Mourad, R.P. 1997. Postmodern interdisciplinarity, *The Review of Higher Education*, 20(2), 113.

Mulgan, G. 2019. *Social Innovation: How Societies Find the Power to Change*, Bristol, Policy Press.

Mulholland, N. 2003. *Google-Books-ID: WQA7DwAAQBAJ. The Cultural Devolution: Art in Britain in the Late Twentieth Century*, London, Routledge.

Myerscough, J. 1988. *The Economic Importance of the Arts in Great Britain*, London, Policy Studies Institute.

Neary, M. 2010. Report. *Student as Producer: Research Engaged Teaching and Learning at the University of Lincoln Userâ€™s Guide 2010–2011*, University of Lincoln. Available at: http://studentasproducer.lincoln.ac.uk/files/2010/11/user-guide.pdf

Neary, M. and Winn, J. 2009. The student as producer: reinventing the student experience in higher education. In *The Future of Higher Education: Policy, Pedagogy and the Student Experience*, Eds L. Bell, H. Stevenson and M. Neary, pp. 192–210, London, Continuum.

Neat, R. 2017. Bet365 chief Denise Coates paid herself £217m last year | Business | The Guardian, *The Guardian*. Available at: https://web.archive.org/web/20171126185631/; https://www.theguardian.com/business/2017/nov/12/bet365-chief-denise-coates-paid-217m-last-year [Accessed 8 June 2021].

Nelson, R. 2013. *Practice as Research in the Arts: Principles, Protocols, Pedagogies, Resistances*, Berlin, Springer Nature.

NESTA. 2016. *Cultural Policy in the Time of the Creative Industries*, London, NESTA.

O'Brien, N., Tanner, W. and Miscampbell, G. 2019. Report. *Onward Thinktank Report: A Question of Degree – Why We Should Cut Graduates' Taxes and Pay for it by Reducing the Number of Low Value University Courses*, London, Onward.

OECD. 2002. *Frascati Manual 2002: Proposed Standard Practice for Surveys on Research and Experimental Development*. The Measurement of Scientific and Technological Activities. [Online]. OECD. Available at: https://www.oecd-ilibrary.org/science-and-technology/frascati-manual-2002_9789264199040-en [Accessed March, 1 2019].

Osterwalder, A. and Pigneur, Y. 2010. *Business Model Generation: A Handbook for Visionaries, Game Changers, and Challengers*, Hoboken, NJ,

John Wiley & Sons. Available at: http://nutsandbolts.mit.edu/2014/resources/businessmodelgeneration_preview.pdf

Oxford Economics. 2020. *The projected economic impact of Covid-19 on the UK creative industries*, Oxford. Available at: https://www.creativeindustriesfederation.com/sites/default/files/inline-images/20200716_OE_Slides_new%20ACE%20data%20-%20Clean%20-%20with%20NEMO%20caveat.pdf [Accessed July 21, 2020].

Patterson, J. and Boehm, C. 2001. CIRCUS for beginners. In *Proceedings of the Conference for Content Integrated Research in Creative User Systems*, [Online], pp. 182–193, Glasgow, University of Glasgow. Available at: http://eprints.staffs.ac.uk/3194/

Petrovic, J. 2019. Philosophy and theory in higher education: Special issue: Imagining the future university. *1*(3), 208.

Quinn, R.-B.M. 2020. *Public Policy and the Arts: A Comparative Study of Great Britain and Ireland: A Comparative Study of Great Britain and Ireland*, 1st ed., p. S.l, London, Routledge.

Rachel, D. 2019. *Don't Look Back in Anger: The Rise and Fall of Cool Britannia, Told by Those Who Were There*, Illustrated ed., London, Trapeze.

REF. 2014. Results & submissions: REF 2014. Available at: https://results.ref.ac.uk/(S(vpxsqffyf3fwjdrv2ynccksd))/Results [Accessed December 30, 2021].

Robinson, K. (2010). Changing Educational Paradigms (RSA Animate), [Online]. Available at: http://comment.rsablogs.org.uk/2010/10/14/rsa-animate-changing-education-paradigms/ [Accessed April 2, 2010].

Rudge, P. 2021. *Beyond the Blue Economy: Creative Industries and Sustainable Development in Small Island Developing States*, 1st ed., London, Routledge.

Rudge, P. 2016. Report. *Framework Strategy for the Staffordshire Moving Image Cluster. Research report for external body*, Stoke-on-Trent, Staffordshire University. Available at: http://eprints.staffs.ac.uk/3741/

Rudy, W. 1984. *The Universities of Europe, 1100–1914 : A History*, Book, Whole, Rutherford, NJ, London; Cranbury, NJ, Associated University Presses.

Rushforth, J. 2017. VCs' salaries – go compare and justify – association of heads of university administration. John Rushforth, Executive Secretary of the Committee of University Chairs (CUC), gives his personal views on the debate around Vice-Chancellors' pay and benefits and discusses the justification of salaries of HE senior leaders. Available at: https://ahua.ac.uk/vcs-salaries-go-compare-justify/ [Accessed October 17, 2017].

Sacco, L. 2014a. Culture 3.0 and its new approach, with Pier Luigi Sacco, *Creative Factory*. Available at: https://vimeo.com/100156465 [Accessed October 18, 2019].

Sacco, L. 2014b. Culture 3.0. ELIA Keynote Talk, European League of Institutes of the Arts.

Sacco, P.L. 2011. Web page. Culture 3.0: A new perspective for the EU 2014–2020 structural funding programming. Available at: http://www.interarts.net/descargas/interarts2577.pdf

Sacco, P.L. 2020. 'There are more things in heaven and earth...' A 'narrative turn' in economics? *Journal of Cultural Economics*. Available at: http://link.springer.com/10.1007/s10824-020-09377-1 [Accessed February 7, 2020].

Savage, J. 2021. The policy and practice of music education in England, 2010–2020, *British Educational Research Journal*, 47(2), 469–483.

Schiemer, G., Sabir, K. and Havryliv, M. 2004. The Pocket Gamelan: A J2ME environment for just intonation. Available at: https://www.researchgate.net/profile/Kenny-Sabir/publication/228809115_The_Pocket_Gamelan_A_j2me_Environment_for_Just_Intonation/links/5524c3500cf22e181e73aae4/The-Pocket-Gamelan-A-j2me-Environment-for-Just-Intonation.pdf?origin=publication_detail

Schrange, M. 2004. *Michael Schrange on Innovation. Interview in Ubiquity, a peer-reviewed Web-based magazine, ACM Publication, December. ubiquity.acm.org.* Available at: http://ubiquity.acm.org

Seipel, M. 2005. Interdisciplinarity: An introduction. Available at: http://mseipel.sites.truman.edu/files/2012/03/Introducing-Interdisciplinarity.pdf [Accessed December 5, 2012].

Smith, C. 1998. *Creative Britain (Former secretary of DCMS)*, London, Faber & Faber.

Snow, C.P. 1964. *The Two Cultures: And a Second Look*, Cambridge, University Press.

Snow, C.P. 1959. *The Two Cultures and the scientific Revolution*, New York, NY, Cambridge University Press.

Sperber, D. 2005. Why Rethink Interdisciplinarity? *Rethinking Inter-disciplinarity*, Interdisciplines. Available at: https://peeps.unet.brandeis.edu/~unsworth/i-majors/Sperber.rethink.pdf

Staffordshire University. 2017. Strategic plan. Available at: https://www.staffs.ac.uk/about/strategic-plan

Steering Group to Education Ministers. 2002. *Review of Arts and Humanities Research Funding: Report of the Steer-Ing Group to Education Ministers*, London. Available at: http://www.education.gov.uk/consultations/downloadable-Docs/SOR_143_1.doc [Accessed February 7, 2012].

Stember, M. 1998. Advancing the social sciences through the interdisciplinary enterprise. In *Interdisciplinarity: Essays from the Literature*, Ed William H. Newell, pp. 337–350, New York, NY, College Entrance Examination Board.

Stephenson, T.J. Bretton Hall College of Higher Education, & National Art Education Archive. 2000. *Performing Arts Education: The Interface between Further and Higher Education Course Provision*, Leeds, Bretton Hall/NAEA.

Sum, N.-L. and Jessop, B. 2013. *Google-Books-ID: z3wtAgAAQBAJ. Towards a Cultural Political Economy: Putting Culture in its Place in Political Economy*, Cheltenham, Edward Elgar Publishing.

TalkRadio. 2019. Boris Johnson will leave EU 'do or die, come what may'. Available at: https://talkradio.co.uk/news/boris-johnson-will-leave-eu-do-or-die-come-what-may-19062531434 [Accessed August 4, 2019].

Team Latestly. 2019. Anti-Trump illustration on border crisis featuring migrant dead father-daughter goes viral, costs Canadian cartoonist his job, *Latestly*. Available at: https://www.latestly.com/world/anti-trump-illustration-on-border-crisis-featuring-migrant-dead-father-daughter-goes-viral-costs-canadian-cartoonist-his-job-973821.html [Accessed August 10, 2019].

Thatcher, M. 2012. *The Downing Street Years*, London, HarperPress.

The Movement for Cultural Democracy. 2018. Rebalancing and redistributing national lottery funding as a step towards a transformative cultural democracy. Available at: https://static1.squarespace.com/static/53fdb85ce4b00f57896789be/t/5c050ee940ec9a8b6f2c9dc8/1543835369887/MCD+REFUNDING+ARTS+%26+CULTURE.pdf [Accessed January 30, 2020].

Thielke, S. 2004. The Hedgehog, the Fox, and the Magister's Pox: Mending the Gap Between Science and the Humanities, *Psychiatric Services*, 55(4), 459–459.

Thomas, D. and Brown, J.S. 2011. *A New Culture of Learning: Cultivating the Imagination for a World of Constant Change*, 1st ed, Charleston, SC, Createspace Independent Publishing Platform.

UK Council for Graduate Education. 1997. *Practice-based Doctorates in the Creative and Performing Arts and Design*, UK Council for Graduate Education. Available at: https://ukcge.ac.uk/assets/resources/4-Practice-based-doctorates-in-the-Creative-and-Performing-Arts1997.pdf

UK Music. 2020. *UK Music Diversity Report 2020. UK Music Diversity*, London, UK MUsic. Available at: https://www.ukmusic.org/equality-diversity/uk-music-diversity-report-2020/ [Accessed February 3, 2021].

UK Parliament. 2009. The evolution of the national curriculum: from Butler to Balls (House of Commons – National Curriculum – Children, Schools and Families Committee). House of Commons - National Curriculum - Children, Schools and Families Committee. Available at: https://publications.parliament.uk/pa/cm200809/cmselect/cmchilsch/344/34405.htm [Accessed August 4, 2021].

UPP Foundation. 2018. *UPP Foundation Civic University Commission Progress Report (The Kerslake Report)*. Available at: https://upp-foundation.org/wp-content/uploads/2018/10/UPP-Foundation-Civic-University-Commission-Progress-Report.pdf

Voluntary Arts. 2020. Common ground: Rewilding the garden. Available at: https://www.voluntaryarts.org/news/commonground [Accessed November 25, 2020].

Walker, H. 2018. The civic university network, *Civic University Network*. Available at: https://civicuniversitynetwork.co.uk/. [Accessed June 9, 2021].

Walton, E. 2014. There's still no such thing as a higher education market, *Times Higher Education (THE)*. Available at: https://www.timeshighereducation.com/comment/opinion/theres-still-no-such-thing-as-a-higher-education-market/2012541.article [Accessed September 23, 2021].

Wang, G., Essl, G., Smith, J., Salazar, S., Cook, P., Hamilton, R., Fiebrink, R., Berger, J., Zhu, D., Ljungstrom, M., Berry, A., Wu, J., Kirk, T., Berger, E. and Segal, J. 2009. SMUE=sonic media: an intersection of the mobile, musical and social. In *SMULE = Sonic Media: An Intersection of the Mobile, Musical, and*

Social, [Online], pp. 283–286, 1 January 2009, Montreal, CA, ICMA. Available at: https://www.researchgate.net/profile/Ge-Wang-18/publication/228939873_SMULE_Sonic_Media_An_Intersection_of_the_Mobile_Musical_and_Social/links/00b4952b01c0441a41000000/SMULE-Sonic-Media-An-Intersection-of-the-Mobile-Musical-and-Social.pdf?origin=publication_detail

Watson, D. 2011. *The Engaged University: International Perspectives on Civic Engagement. International studies in Higher Education,* New York, NY, Routledge.

Watson, D. 2014. *The Question of Conscience: Higher Education and Personal Responsibility* Bedford Way papers Book, Whole. London, Institute of Education Press.

Watson, D. 2009. *The Question of Morale: Managing Happiness and Unhappiness in University Life,* Maidenhead, McGraw-Hill. Available at: http://www.NCL.eblib.com/patron/FullRecord.aspx?p=487791

Wikipedia Contributors. 2021a. BBC television, *Wikipedia.* Available at: https://en.wikipedia.org/w/index.php?title=BBC_Television&oldid=1062819483 [Accessed January 2, 2022].

Wikipedia Contributors. 2019. Dominic cummings, *Wikipedia.* Available at: https://en.wikipedia.org/w/index.php?title=Dominic_Cummings&oldid=909295784 [Accessed August 4, 2019].

Wikipedia Contributors. 2021b. Telecinema, *Wikipedia.* Available at: https://en.wikipedia.org/w/index.php?title=Telecinema&oldid=1039025994 [Accessed January 3, 2022].

Williamson, G. 2021a. Gavin Williamson (secretary of state for education): Skills, jobs and freedom. My priorities for this week's Queen's speech – and the year ahead. Conservative Home. Available at: https://www.conservativehome.com/platform/2021/05/gavin-williamson-skills-jobs-and-freedom-my-priorities-for-this-weeks-queens-speech-and-the-year-ahead.html [Accessed June 8, 2021].

Williamson, G. 2021b. Notification to the Office for Students (OfS) by the Secretary of State for Education to set terms and conditions for the allocation by OfS of Strategic Priorities Grant funding for the 2021/22 Academic Year. Available at: https://www.officeforstudents.org.uk/media/0e833c6f-c355-4743-8953-071bbe9b1518/ts-and-cs-onrecurrent-funding-19-july.pdf

Wilson, N., Gross, J. and Bull, A. 2016. Towards cultural democracy: promoting cultural capabilities for everyone. Towards-cultural-democracy. Available at: https://www.kcl.ac.uk/Cultural/-/Projects/

Winn, J. 2015. The co-operative university: Labour, property and pedagogy, *Power and Education*, 7(1), 39–55.

Woodin, T. 2015. *Co-operation, Learning and Co-operative Values: Contemporary Issues in Education*, London and New York, NY, Routledge.

Wright, S. and Shore, C. Eds. 2017. *Death of the Public University? Uncertain Futures for Higher Education in the Knowledge Economy*, 1st ed., New York, NY, Berghahn.

Wright, S., Greenwood, D. and Boden, R. 2011. Report on a field visit to Mondragón University: a cooperative experience/experiment, *Learning and Teaching: The International Journal of Higher Education in the Social Sciences (LATISS)*, 4(3), 38–56.

INDEX